Deadly Fever

Deadly Fever

Racism, Disease and a Media Panic

Charles T. Adeyanju

Fernwood Publishing • Halifax and Winnipeg

Dedicated to the memory of my grandmother:
Juliana Ajayi Alonge
(a teacher of humility, humaneness and contentment)

Editing: Jessica Antony
Cover design: John van der Woude
Printed and bound in Canada by Hignell Book Printing

Mixed Sources
Product group from well-managed
forests and other controlled sources
www.fsc.org   Cert no. SW-COC-003438
© 1996 Forest Stewardship Council

Published in Canada by Fernwood Publishing
32 Oceanvista Lane
Black Point, Nova Scotia, B0J 1B0
and #8 - 222 Osborne Street, Winnipeg, Manitoba, R3L 1Z3
www.fernwoodpublishing.ca

Fernwood Publishing Company Limited gratefully acknowledges the financial support of the
Government of Canada through the Canada Book Fund, the Canada Council for the Arts, the
Nova Scotia Department of Tourism and Culture and the Province of Manitoba, through the
Book Publishing Tax Credit, for our publishing program.

Library and Archives Canada Cataloguing in Publication

Adeyanju, Charles T., 1969-
Deadly fever : racism, disease and a medic panic / Charles T. Adeyanju.

ISBN 978-1-55266-341-7

1. Health and race--Canada--Case studies. 2. Racism--Health
aspects--Canada--Case studies. 3. Minority women--Medical
care--Canada--Case studies. 4. Immigrants--Medical care--Canada--Case
studies. 5. Discrimination in medical care--Canada--Case studies. I. Title.

RA564.86.A34 2010   362.1'0820971   C2010-900016-1

Contents

Acknowledgements

This book evolved from a doctoral dissertation: I owe many a debt of gratitude in the course of researching and writing the book.

My understanding of media and society was shaped by others during my doctoral research program. For this, I am grateful to Vic Satzewich, James Gillett, Garry Warner and Graham Knight, all of whom provided scholarly advice and intellectual stimulation throughout the collection and analysis of data that appears in this book. I am also thankful to Jackie Tucker, Corinne Jehle and Olga Cannon, administrative staff at McMaster University's Department of Sociology, for their kindness throughout the duration of my doctoral research program.

I would not have survived a doctoral program without the support I received from my family. I am beholden to my parents, Patrick Oso Adeyanju Adedipe and Victoria Oluremi Adeyanju, for their prayers and unflinching support for my venture into postgraduate studies; my son, Ayden Oso Adeyanju-Jackson, and his mum Shannon Jackson, for their understanding throughout the researching and writing of the book; my sister Omowande Cecilia Osidein and her family, who accommodated my son and me in their Toronto apartment on our regular visits during the collection and analysis of data for the book; and my sisters Olubunmi Maria Akinsanya and Mercy Adenike Fajana and uncle Satide Oroko for their well wishes.

Tolu Adewumi, Donald Fajemisin and Timothy Olusola Adeyanju were morally supportive of my decision to write the book. For this I am appreciative.

Special thanks to the members of Hamilton's Black community who participated in the study. Their "re-living" of an unfortunate incident made the research possible. Some members of the Black community declined my request to participate in the research; I am equally grateful to them, as it made me understand the degree of devastation the "Ebola story" wrought on them and their community. To the journalists and members of the medical community who enthusiastically took part in the study, I thank you.

I must acknowledge my colleagues at the University of Prince Edward Island (UPEI), who received me with open arms on my arrival to join the Department of Sociology and Anthropology as a faculty member this past summer. Professor Joe Kopachevsky, Dr. Jean Mitchell, Dr. Udo Krautwurst, Dr. Benet Davetian, Dr. Antonio Sorge, Dr. Judy-Lynn Richards, Professor James Rodd and Ms. Eleanor-Anne Nahrgang, of the Department of Sociology and Anthropology, and Dr. Pamela Courtney-Hall of the Philosophy Department, fostered a welcoming environment that made the timely completion of this book possible.

Many read the manuscript and provided insightful comments on all or parts of it at various stages of its preparation. I am especially grateful to Janet Ngo, Tope Oriola, Tamari Kitossa and Nicole Neverson for drawing my attention to relevant academic sources and for reading the earlier drafts of the manuscript. Tope Oriola encouraged me to put the "Ebola story" in writing for public awareness. For this, I also give him thanks. Special acknowledgments go to the two anonymous reviewers for Fernwood Publishing for their constructive criticism and insightful comments on the manuscript. Words are not enough to express my gratitude to Jessica Antony and Wayne Antony for their editorial skills, guidance and incisive comments throughout the entire publication process. Thanks as well to Fernwood's production staff: Debbie Mathers for pre-production, Beverley Rach for layout and page design, Brenda Conroy for proofreading and John van der Woude for cover design. I should say that I am fully responsible for any errors and omissions.

Preface

After the well-publicized non-Ebola[1] panic in Canada in the winter of 2001, many kept asking how the case was brought to a close. "Did she have Ebola?" was the question asked by many during my data collection and preparation of material for this book. If I answered "No," the follow up question was, "What did she have?" As a matter of fact, some did believe that the "African woman" who was the focus of media coverage brought the deadly Ebola virus to Canada but that public health intervention contained its spread. This partial and inaccurate understanding of the event might have stemmed from the way the Ebola incident was reported by the media. The media seemed to sensationalize and over-dramatize the case while implicating issues of race and immigration. Disappointingly, the media were insensitive to the impact of their style of reporting on the Black community and its influence on members of the Canadian public who reduced the incident to an immigration/race problem. The media paid little to no attention to how the panic they incited was experienced by members of the Black community. For the majority of the Black community the non-Ebola panic was an unfortunate incident that further perpetuated racism against Blacks and new immigrants to Canada.

This book is a comprehensive account of the non-Ebola incident, situated in the broader literature on race, racism and racialization in Canadian society. It specifically shows how race as an organizing principle of contemporary society has been sustained by the Canadian press. The book also shows the resilience of racism in a modern liberal democratic society that professes equality, human rights and justice. The book describes the role of mass media in using the Ebola story to perpetuate racial stratification.

Canadians knew about the Ebola case through the prism of the mass media and *ipso facto* were exposed to a partially ideologically inflected perspective. The media account was skewed and unbalanced. This book is all-encompassing in its account of the incident. It presents perspectives from the journalists and medical practitioners, as juxtaposed with members of the Black community. This book speaks for members of the Black community, giving them a voice. As one of the newspapers that devotedly covered the incident marked the one-year anniversary of the event by awarding one of its journalists, the men, women and children of the Black community shuddered. They shuddered for the association of a deadly disease with their community; they shuddered for what they perceived as a "celebration" of their "persecution." The media's commemoration cum celebration of the event turned a journalist into a heroine, while the woman at the centre of the coverage and the community she was associated with were transmuted into villains. With the celebration, racism seemed to disappear in what Razack (2004: 7) refers to as the "national memory." For the journalists, the coverage is not about race/ethnicity. It is about rescuing the nation from catastrophe. So, as in Razack's (2004: 7) philippic reaction to Canadian peacekeeping occupation in Africa, "race disappears from public memory through a variety of tricks, and incidents of racial violence become transformed into something else, something we can live with." The non-Ebola case was not something that the Black community "can live with" because their denigration in the Canadian public remains in their collective memory even though their resilience in the face of everyday challenges is nonpareil. In fact, members of the Black community were strengthened by the incident, but they will never forget.

I am concerned that we are not moving forward fast enough in our race relations in this country. At the official multiculturalism policy level, there is profession of equality, but in everyday reality the relationships of superior and subordinate continue to exist between racial minorities and the dominant White population in Canadian society. These unequal relations are sustained by key institutions of Canadian society. The turn of the twenty-first century witnessed sporadic incidents of racial profiling (see Tator and Henry 2006) targeting racial minorities in our country. The non-Ebola case in the winter of 2001 targeted Blacks; the terrorist attacks on the World Trade Center and the Pentagon in September 2001 resulted in overt anti-Muslim and anti-Arab sentiments at interpersonal and institutional levels; and the severe acute respiratory syndrome (SARS) pointed the finger at the Chinese. As anti-immigrant sentiments grow in times of crisis and in times of peace, many social activists are becoming concerned that racism may be becoming normalized in Canadian society.

Some may be wondering about my subject position in conceiving and writing this book. I wrote the book as a scholar and as a member of the Black community. Most importantly, I wrote the book as a concerned citizen of the world. In spite of my proclivity to take particular points of view because of my subject position as an African and a first generation Canadian immigrant with the burning desire for permanently resolving the problem of racial inequality that exists in this country, I adhere strongly to Becker's (1967) recommendation that, "to make sure that, whatever point of view we take, our research meets the standards of good scientific work, that our unavoidable sympathies do not render our results invalid" (Becker 1967: 46). The book is derived from vigorous social scientific research that spanned a period of two years.

Racism is obviously one of the major pernicious social problems of our time. This book is recommended for the victims of racism, racist victimizers, anti-racists and those who are on the fence in the fight against racism. One of the aims of the book is to make all realize that racism attenuates the shared humanity of the victimized and the victimizers. Just as the oppressed suffer, so are the oppressors hostage of hatred and ignorance. As Nelson Mandela (1994: 544) states in his peroration, "A man who takes away another man's freedom is a prisoner of hatred, he is locked behind the bars of prejudice and narrow mindedness...the oppressed and the oppressor alike are robbed of their humanity."

The book is organized in six chapters. Chapter 1 provides context for the book by giving an overview of the case study and an examination of ethno-racial relations in Canadian society. The non-Ebola narrative is set in the context of broader historical and contemporary actualities of ethnic and racial relations in Canada. The chapter also discusses the methodology employed to collect data for the book. Chapter 2 reviews the literature that forms the theoretical backdrop for the study. Chapter 3 is substantive: it largely deals with the content analysis of four of the newspapers that covered the non-Ebola story. The translation of a health risk into an immigration and race problem by the media is crucial to the chapter. Chapter 4 discusses the competing claims of medical practitioners of Congolese descent and lay members of the Black community as well as the views of journalists and medical practitioners who played varying roles in the case. Chapter 5 of the book focuses on the narratives of members of the Black community in Hamilton, or what Henry (2006: 170) refers to as "the subjective testimonials of people who are aggrieved, hurt, and disadvantaged by racism." The chapter documents the experiences of members of the Black community and their interpretations of media coverage of the non-Ebola case. Finally, chapter 6 recaps the findings of the study and suggests socio-economic integration of racial minorities and new immigrants as a panacea for the social problem of racialization and racism.

Note

1. This case is referred to as "non-Ebola," given that there was no actual incident of Ebola. Nevertheless, the coverage generated a panic.

Chapter 1

Canada: A Racialized Past

A source said one of the community members who might be at risk attends a downtown Hamilton school. A staff member at Ecole Notre Dame, a French elementary school, said they have two students who recently arrived from Congo — but neither had been contacted by public-health officials. In Hamilton there are as many as 300 residents originally from the Democratic Republic of Congo, according to a representative for the Settlement and Integration Services Organization. (*Globe and Mail*, February 8, 2001a)

Immigration officials are investigating whether a Congolese woman who started an Ebola scare in Southern Ontario last month is a courier for a diamond smuggling ring. A Quebec man who was to host the woman during her stay in Canada is believed to have transferred US $100,000 to a Kinshasa company called Isocool prior to her arrival. (*National Post*, March 3, 2001)

Hamilton is a southwestern Ontario town that has undergone social and economic transformation over time. It was one of the leading manufacturing towns of iron and steel until the decline of these industries in the 1980s (Livingstone and Magan 1996: 4–5). Hamilton, like many other Canadian metropolises, is ethnically and racially diverse. However, its ethno-racial diversity is not devoid of the social problem of racial intolerance that confronts other Canadian cities (Smith 2003). The possibility of an Ebola-positive patient from the Democratic Republic of Congo, on a visitor's visa, being admitted to a hospital in Hamilton first appeared in the print media on February 6, 2001. Newspapers indicated that while the woman was visiting an acquaintance in Hamilton on February 4, 2001, she fell ill: she was feeling unwell, could not eat and had a rising fever. According to her hostess, as reported in the newspaper stories, that Sunday night an ambulance was requested to transport her to the Henderson Hospital in Hamilton. Under medical examination, Ebola was considered as a probable cause of her illness by the medical practitioners who attended to her. The *Globe and Mail* of February 7, 2001, quoting a source familiar with the case, reported that on Monday, February 5, the woman's illness had become so severe that she was "bleeding from several sites on the body." Newspaper reports indicated that the symptoms exhibited by the woman, coupled with her travel history, made doctors suspect the Ebola virus as the probable cause of her illness. After a series of tests, however, Ebola was ruled out.

This book is about the Canadian media's articulation of the suspected infectious disease with race and immigration and the resilience of the racialized Other to their representations in the media. Using the media coverage of the female Congolese visitor to Canada suspected of the serious contagious disease, the maintenance of race as an organizing principle in Canadian society is illustrated.[1] This study highlights the contradictions between the "ideals" of equality and the "reality" of inequality in Canadian society. Canada is a democratic modern society with the ideals of equality and freedom, yet there is race-based inequality (Bolaria and Li 1985; Mensah 2002; Henry and Tator 2006). This case study contributes to the scholarship on the discrepancies between those ideals of freedom and equality espoused in Canadian society and the realities and experiences of racism by Canada's visible minorities by focusing on the media's role in fanning an ember of racism in their representation of a non-Ebola[2] panic. This book is not only about the panic caused by media representation but also about how the panic was experienced by the Black community. The non-Ebola case was a proxy for expressing the anxiety and concern of Canadians over the growing presence of non-Europeans in this country. The media used the case as an analogy of all that is considered threatening to Canadian society, especially criminality, racial impurity, immigration and scarce social resources.

Canada has a racialized history of immigration (Bolaria and Li 1985; Li 1998; Li 2003). It has a recent history of excluding "peripheral Europeans" (Satzewich 2000) and non-Whites from immigrating to Canada. Satzewich (1991) documented different standards used by the Canadian state to incorporate different ethnic and racial groups in the post-war era. Throughout the history of Canadian immigration, race was one of the key ways that Canadians made sense of Self and their social world. Stanley Barrett (1994: 270) cannot be more explicit on this fact when he states that Canadians have a "racial capacity." The framing of the non-Ebola case in the media and interviews conducted with journalists affirm that many Canadians perceive the growing ethno-racial diversity in Canada, since the de-racialized immigration policy of the 1960s, as a challenge to Euro-Canadian hegemony (Hier and Greenberg 2002; Li 2003). The folkloric conception of Canada as "White" in Canadians' day-to-day living is shattered by the growing mosaic of cultures and "races." I argue that the non-Ebola case was a reaction to this dramatic change and that the media coverage of the case as a racial/immigration problem could only resonate with an audience that used the idea of race to make sense of its world.

The Non-Ebola Case

Ebola is a virus named after a river in the Democratic Republic of Congo, formerly known as Zaire, where it was first recognized in 1976. Subsequent outbreaks occurred in the Democratic Republic of Congo in 1977; Sudan in 1979; Gabon in 1994 and 1996; Democratic Republic of Congo in 1995; Uganda in 2000–2001; and on the border of Gabon and the Democratic Republic of Congo in 2001–2002. The Ebola virus and the Marburg virus are two members of a family of viruses called "filoviridae," and they can cause severe hemorrhagic fever in humans and nonhuman primates. The etiology of Ebola is unknown. In the realist sense of risk (see Lupton 1999), the Ebola virus can be deadly; its mortality rate ranges from 50 to 90 percent. While Ebola is very lethargic, its spread is highly localized.

Joffe and Haarhoff (2002) refer to Ebola as one of the "far-flung illnesses" because it breaks out in places that are geographically remote from the West. However, members of Western societies are aware of Ebola through the mass media (Ungar 1998). Based on Western media coverage of the Ebola outbreak in Zaire (now Democratic Republic of Congo) in 1995, Ungar (1998) argues that in the early stage of the coverage, Ebola was constructed as very deadly or in a "mutation-contagion" phase, but after a few days the media allayed the fear of the Western public by reporting that Ebola was an African problem and was of no danger to the Western audience. Allaying the fear of the Western audience is accomplished through what he refers to as the "containment package." Ungar's (1998) study makes one realize that Canadians had some knowledge of Ebola as a deadly disease prior to the breaking news of a possible presence of Ebola in Canada in the winter of 2001. The news coverage of a suspected Ebola case tapped into Canadians' pre-existing knowledge of Ebola as a deadly disease and created fear and anxiety, but it was the association of the disease with a foreign ecology in prior and current media coverage that reinforced racial discrimination in a segment of the population.

The local newspaper, the *Hamilton Spectator*, a widely read newspaper in Hamilton and the surrounding area, published stories on how a panic-stricken community was reacting to the news of Ebola in their neighbour-hoods. According to the *Hamilton Spectator*'s and other news media reports, the situation had become serious enough that those who came in contact with the woman, including five ambulance workers, were immediately identified for isolation; the ambulances in which she was transported were taken out of service; and some hospital staff who came in contact with the patient voluntarily quarantined themselves to protect their family members from contracting the virus.

As the media placed emphasis on Ebola as the possible cause of the patient's illness in their coverage, public reaction in the Hamilton area grew.

The Heritage Front, a self-acclaimed White supremacist group, picketed the hospital and distributed racist pamphlets in the vicinity of the hospital; hospital workers panicked and threatened legal action against the hospital for exposing them to danger; Black children in some elementary schools in Hamilton were shunned by their fellow White students; and an acquaintance of the patient in the Congolese community is reported to have lost jobs and moved out of her residence.

Subsequent newspaper articles reported that after a series of medical tests, Ebola and other suspected hemorrhagic fevers were ruled out. As soon as Ebola and these other hemorrhagic fevers were ruled out by the medical experts, the news quickly dropped off the media radar, just as suddenly as it was brought to light. But then news reports brought to public attention that the woman's medical care had been costly and also that she was being investigated by the authorities for diamond smuggling.

For members of the Black community in Hamilton, the coverage of the event by the media was not only racist but fanned an ember of racist prejudice and discrimination in the community. They deplored the implied relationship between the suspected disease, immigration and race. Members of the Black community also felt that the disclosure and publication of the patient's name and the display of photographs of where she stayed was "un-Canadian," that is, she was singled out for special treatment because of her racial background. They also expressed dissatisfaction over the way that the hospital and its physicians handled the case. Murdocca's (2003: 29) comments on the case offer an insight that is congruent to the feelings of frustration expressed by members of the Black community in Hamilton:

> It is imperative to point out that the conceptual link that the Heritage Front made between a Congolese visitor and racialized immigrants and refugees from "high risk" areas is the same connection made by immigration officials, medical experts, journalists and those who wrote letters to the editor. Instead of producing incompatible versions of the threat of contagious disease, the ideological intersections of "far right" organizations, mainstream media and medical and government officials suggest that these seemingly disparate political agendas in fact promote analogous agendas that use racialized bodies as vectors of disease as their narrative core.

The non-Ebola case raises a set of questions relating to identity, race, racialization, racism, immigration, insecurity and safety. This book aims to answer three questions. What is the Canadian media coverage of Ebola in the winter of 2001? How was the non-Ebola case explained by journalists, physicians and members of the Black community? How was the non-Ebola panic experienced and constructed by members of the Black community? Apart from addressing the issues of the *mechanisms* of media representation and the *effects* of the coverage on a segment of the population, this book situates the case within the larger literature on Canadian immigration, race, racial categorization and heath panics. The major thrust of the point sustained throughout the book is that the non-Ebola case was used by the media as a proxy for expressing the anxiety and insecurity that Canadians feel over the changing racial composition of Canada.

Immigration, Race and the Imagined Canadian Nation

The non-Ebola narratives can be placed in the larger context of significa-tion of race and its cross-articulation with social problems not only in news reporting but also in everyday life in Canada (Henry and Tator 2002, 2006). The concepts of racism, racialization and race are germane to the process of "Othering" the social problems of crime (Henry and Tator 2002: 163–204; Tator and Henry 2006), "illegal" migration (Hier and Greenberg 2001, 2002), deception (Pratt and Valverde 2002) and infectious diseases (Power 1995; Ungar 1998; Joffe and Haarhoff 2002; Washer 2004) in Western societies.

Social scientists conceive of race as a label that has been employed to differentiate human beings on the basis of skin colour or culture (Satzewich 1998b; Miles and Brown 2003). According to Miles and Brown (2003: 88–89), race is a product of "signification." That is, it is the attribution of meaning to "certain somatic characteristics," most especially skin colour. The biological definition of race did not emerge until the late eighteenth and early nineteenth centuries, but by the second half of the twentieth century, an essentialist definition of race in terms of biology had been rejected in social science. Classifying human beings into different races has never been fortuitous because the race idiom has always served the purpose of including the "desirables" and excluding the "undesirables." Although social scientists have discredited the biological basis of race, it has remained one of the fundamental coordinates of modern societies.

Historically, race was an imposition on the Other, but it has not always exclusively been a discourse of oppression. In the words of Miles and Brown (2003: 91):

> During the twentieth century, those who have been its object have often accepted their designation as a biologically distinct and discreet population, as a "race," but have inverted the negative evaluation of their character and capacities. Consequently, the discourse of "race" has been transformed into a discourse of resistance. Certain somatic characteristics (usually skin color) have been signified as the founda-tion for a common experience and fate as an excluded population, irrespective of class position and cultural origin.

Miles and Brown (2003: 101) define racialization as "those instances where social relations between people have been structured by the signification of human biological characteristics in such a way as to define and construct differentiated collectivities." Racialization entails the attribution of social meanings to somatic variations in a human population. Satzewich (1998b: 32) presents this point more clearly by stating that the "process of racialization is the delineation of group boundaries and identities by reference to physical and/or genetic criteria or by reference to the term race." Racialization is a "dialectical process," that is, "to define the Other necessarily entails defining 'Self' by the same criteria" (Miles and Brown 2003: 101). Whereas racism is about negative evaluation of racialized Others, racialization is not necessarily racist because people can classify themselves or be classified by others on the basis of physical or cultural characteristics without imputing negative meanings to the categories. As Satzewich (1998b: 34–35) points out, many Canadians use the marker of race to categorize themselves or others without necessarily being racist. It is not the classification that is problematic (Hall 1996) but the advantages that classifications confer on one collectivity at the expense of another.

As has been pointed out above, races of people do not exist in a biological sense, but people think and behave as though they exist. People hold racist prejudices and single others out based on the notion that they are biologically different. There is no agreed upon definition of racism (see Satzewich 1998b: 34–36), but most social scientists would not dispute the fact that racism is grounded in a belief of a natural sub-division of the human population into discreet races that can be ranked hierarchically. Racism is therefore a form of racialization that conceives of the world as having multiple races, and one or more of the races identified "must be attributed with additional (negatively evaluated) characteristics and/or must be represented as inducing negative consequences for (an)other group(s)" (Miles and Brown 2003: 104). Racism may select either cultural or biological characteristics in a population as the basis for singling out the Other for special treatment.

Martin Barker (1981) uses the concept of "new racism" to distinguish the contemporary strain of racism from the old-fashioned racism. Rather than focusing on biological superiority of one race, the former dwells on cultural superiority of one collectivity over others. Barker (1981) alludes to the expression of anti-immigrant sentiments by British politicians in the 1970s as instances of racism. He states that the new form of racism does not talk about 'race' as the ranking of human collectivities in a pecking order on the basis of skin colour. Rather, hierarchies of groups are expressed in terms of cultural differences. Thus, he describes the concept of the new racism as a theory of human nature. Human nature is such that it is natural to form a bounded community, a nation, aware of its differences from other nations. They are not better or worse. But feelings of antagonism will be aroused if outsiders are admitted. And there grows up a special form of connection between a nation and the place it lives. (Barker 1981: 21)

Barker's idea of new racism provides an interesting insight into understanding the currents and undercurrents of contemporary racism. Most importantly, it points out that an attitude or behaviour does not necessarily have to be grounded in biological discourse to qualify as racist.

All in all, the ideas of race, racialization, racism and new racism inform the classification of the human population and have patterned relationships between and among groups of people in modern societies. These notions of race, racialization, racism and new racism have played a major role in organizing social relations in the historical formation of Canada.[3] Bolaria and Li (1985), for example, document the differential incorporation of non-European immigrants into Canada in the period before 1962. The discrimination against immigrants from Asia and the Caribbean was racial in the sense that they were exploited in the labour market and were excluded from circulating freely in the labour market and becoming members of the "Canadian imagined community." In the case of the Chinese, their immigration to Canada before 1923 was mainly based on the intermittent labour demand of the Canadian economy. Their immigration started around 1858, when some of them came from the west coast of the U.S. to work in the gold mines of Fraser Valley in British Columbia. Subsequent Chinese immigration, directly from China, followed between 1881 and 1885, during the construction of the Canadian Pacific Railway (CPR) (Bolaria and Li 1985). Couched in a strict political economy perspective, Bolaria and Li (1985) argue that anti-Chinese sentiments expressed by the public and the Canadian state were induced by their presumed competition with White workers in times of surplus labour supply. To prevent the Chinese from competing with Canadian workers, anti-Chinese bills were passed by both the provincial legislature and the federal parliament. When the CPR was completed in 1885, a head tax of $50 was imposed upon Chinese entering Canada (Bolaria and Li 1985). The Chinese head tax was increased to $100 in 1900, and to $500 in 1903. In 1923, the Canadian parliament passed the Chinese Immigration Act, which barred all Chinese from entering the country. This racist ban was not lifted until 1947.

The role of the Canadian state in differentially incorporating immigrants into Canadian society after the Second World War is extensively discussed by Satzewich (1991). According to Satzewich, post-war immigration to Canada was driven by the Canadian state's notion of Canadian identity. While Bolaria and Li (1985) consider labour need as the main variable driving the immigration policy at the time in question, Satzewich (1991), based on a mode of incorporation typology of "free immigration," "unfree immigration" and "unfree migration," posits that it was a combination of economic, cultural and ideological factors. Thus, people of European descent were allowed to immigrate to Canada based on the criterion of their perceived cultural and physiological similarities with "Canadians." The Dutch, British and Germans gained access to Canada as free immigrants. They were expected to become naturalized Canadians after five years of residence in Canada. The Polish and those of Southern and Eastern European descent were incorporated as unfree immigrants. They arrived in Canada under certain conditions and, after three years of residency, could circulate freely in the labour market and become naturalized Canadians. In Satzewich's (1991) study, Blacks constituted the unfree migrant category. They were only allowed to migrate to Canada on conditions that precluded them from becoming permanent Canadian residents. Caribbean farm workers were classified as "unfree migrant labour" because "they have been defined as temporary entrants to Canada without the right of permanent settlement, and because it is not intended that they become citizens of the country and parts of the imagined community of the Canadian nation" (Satzewich 1991: 111).

In what Satzewich (1991: 116) referred to as the "racialization of permanent settlement," the Canadian state separated labour force renewal from labour force maintenance: the migrant's family is left in the Caribbean, exonerating the Canadian state from assuming responsibilities for the physical reproduction of the worker's family and reproduction costs of the labourer when he/she is unemployed. Satzewich (1991) finds that the differential incorporation of Blacks, compared to European migrant labourers, into Canadian society stemmed from exploitation but was also motivated by the imagined conception of Canada as a society of White people. Thus he argues that the barring of Black migrants from assuming permanent resident status is blatantly racist:

> They were defined as unable to "assimilate," unable to adjust to the Canadian climate, and as the cause of potential social and "racial" problems in the country, all of which were negatively associated characteristics linked to "race." Very generally, "black" people were not allowed to become members of the Canadian imagined community. (Satzewich 1991: 128)

From the public policy perspective, in the period before 1962, it was overtly expressed that Black immigration could constitute a risk to Canada. Canadian public officials often referred to their notion of threat in terms of a race relations problem, which they claimed had gestated in the U.K. and the U.S. Anxieties over racial diversity at the time were expressed by a high level public functionary. Satzewich (1991: 139) notes:

> It should also be mentioned here that one of the policy factors was a concern over the long range wisdom of a substantial increase in negro immigration to Canada. The racial problems of Britain and the United States undoubtedly influenced this concern which still exists today.

Unfree immigrants also experienced racialization because of their cultural difference from the French and the British. In a different study by Satzewich (2000), "European ethnics" as varied as Italians, Ukrainians, Greeks, Polish and Irish are referred to as "peripheral Europeans" because of their racialized experiences in North America in the late nineteenth and early twentieth centuries. In his assessment, Satzewich (2000: 275) observes that some scholars tend to "fall back on old essentialist and reified understandings of 'race.'" He uses the experiences of racism by "peripheral Europeans" to show that the ontology of race is a social construction. Whiteness was an achieved status, and European ethnics could choose to be non-White. In an example of the former, the Irish did not automatically qualify as White; they fought and struggled to become White. On the other hand, Ukrainians made their national identity a priority over a White racial identity.[4]

In the 1960s, the Canadian immigration policy was de-racialized owing to the need for skilled labour, not enough of which was was available from Europe, and an aversion to racism worldwide. As a result, immigrants of non-European descent were allowed to immigrate to Canada based on a universal points system. The points system assessed prospective immigrants on "objective criteria," such as age, skills, education and language proficiency. Since then, Canada has experienced growth in immigration from non-traditional sources such as Asia, Africa, the Caribbean and Latin America. The next section discusses the growth of the non-European population in Canada, public perceptions of racial diversity and the reaction of the Canadian population.

Racial Diversity, Anxieties and Racial Categorization

Since the de-racialized immigration policy of the 1960s, Canada has experienced immigration from the non-traditional sources of Asia and Africa. As a result, anxieties have emerged among the Canadian public around the changing nature of the racial composition of Canada (Li 2003). Familiar social spaces, such as neighbourhoods, workplaces and schools are becoming racially diverse due to immigration from non-European countries. Consequently, there are growing feelings of insecurity and unease as racial diversity is considered a challenge to Euro-Canadian supremacy (see Creese and Peterson 1996; Hier and Greenberg 2002). Concerns and anxieties over immigration have also been expressed in other Western industrial societies during the past few decades. They have been expressed in the form of racist backlash and anti-immigration sentiments in the public speeches of politicians (see Barker 1981) and in the media. In the contemporary West, crass anti-immigrant sentiments, or what Husbands (1994) refers to as the "new moral panics," are not unconnected to shifting broader social, historical, economic and cultural conditions of "late modern societies"[5] (Wodak and Matouschek 1993; Zong 1994; Simmons 1998a, 1998b; Hier and Greenberg 2002).

Li (2003) distinguishes between racial and ethnic diversities in the Canadian context. He argues that, as an immigrant country, Canada has always been linguistically, ethnically and culturally heterogeneous but that it was not until the de-racialized immigration program of the 1960s that racial minorities became visible. Li argues that the growing presence of people of non-European descent, distinguished by their discernible physical features, has become a source of anxiety for White Canadians. Over time, the growing population of non-Europeans has shifted the boundary of who is "White"to include groups such as Italians, Greeks, Irish and Ukrainians, who were once constructed as the Other in relation to "White Europeans" (see Porter 1965; Satzewich 2000).

At the early stage, during the period before the 1960s, there was a deterministic relationship between racial identity and socio-economic location in most Western industrial societies. Since the 1960s there has been no *necessary* association between class location and cultural background under the regime of what Miles and Satzewich refer to as "postmodern capitalism" (1990). As in the analysis of Simmons (1998b) of post-1960s Asian immigrants in Canada, many recent Asian immigrants have overcome their confinement to low-wage and dangerous jobs. Their pre-migration affluence has enabled them to challenge old stereotypes. However, this has generated what Simmons (1998b) calls "reactive racism," a replacement of old racist stereotypes. Simmons (1998b: 47) states that "contemporary racism is based on the stigmatization of people who cannot be faulted in terms of their work-ethic or productive contributions." It is "reactive," as it is based increasingly on resentment against more affluent and successful immigrants. Issues of concern are diverse and rest "on cultural biases, fears, distortions and misunderstandings" (Simmons 1998b: 47). In spite of empirical evidence to show that new immigrants challenge old racist stereotypes with their relatively high education, skills and capital acumen (in the case of some Chinese, for example), ethno-racial background still largely accounts for social and economic inequalities in Canadian society (see Li 1998; Ornstein 2000; Galabuzi 2006).

Using Porter's (1965) charter groups (the French and British) as the reference point, Li (2003) claims that Canada in 1991 was no more diverse than it was in 1961, considering that the population of those who were not of British or French origin made up around 26 to 28 percent between 1961 and 1991 (Li 2003: 128). However, empirical data show that there was an increase in the number of people of non-European origin in Canada: in 1971 those of African origin comprised less than 1 percent of those not of British or French origin, whereas by 1991 they accounted for 3.4 percent. Similarly, those of Asian origin rose from 5 percent of those not of French or British origin in 1971 to 11.3 percent in 1981, and to 21.6 percent in 1991 (Li 2003: 128). Based on these figures, Li insists that the non-White category of the population still remains a numeric minority in Canada. Accordingly, Africans and Asians only constituted about one-quarter of the 55 percent of non-British and non-French origin of the Canadian population in the 1991 census; and those of the Pacific Islands and Latin American origins accounted for 2.5 percent of non-British and non-French origin (Li 2003: 128). Based on this empirical indicator, Li states that it is not so much the increase in the non-British and non-French presence in Canada that makes ethnic diversity more noticeable in Canada, but the growth of racial minorities within the category of non-British and non-French Europeans (Li 2003: 128).

Li also claims that the perception that there is too much cultural diversity and the assertion that Canadian identity is compromised by immigration are very dubious. He argues that Canada is still largely European in its cultural orientation. In his words:

> It appears that much of the reservation towards diversity being expressed in the immigration discourse is based on race and on the perception of some long-time Canadians that non-white immigrants mean unbridgeable differences. It is not the growing number of non-white immigrants in Canadian cities that is challenging the social cohesion. Rather, it is the ideological interpretation of "race" and "colour" as implying fundamental and undesirable differences that is seen as challenging the normative tradition of Canada, one that is based on the cultural balance between the British and the French, and one that is characteristically European in flavour. (Li 2003: 129)

In view of the brief historical and contemporary accounts of Canadian immigration policy and ethno-racial relations in Canada laid out above, it goes without saying that the Canadian media participate in setting the public context for anti-racial-diversity sentiments and play an important role in the contemporary racialization of immigration and diversity. The construction of the non-Ebola case in the media around immigration and racial diversity could be said to have tapped into the existing sense of insecurity and anxiety resulting from social and cultural changes that are confronting Canadians. The media do not exist in a social, political and economic vacuum. Through history, immigration and colonialism, Canadians have acquired what Giddens (1984: 4) refers to as the "mutual knowledge incorporated in encounters," which the Canadian press drew on. In this case, the idea of a "contagious" African re-affirmed the pre-existing knowledge of the fundamental difference between Self and Other. Canadians did not need to be told by the media that there are different races. They just needed to be reminded.

Mass Media and Racial Representations

For many members of modern societies, their knowledge of social reality comes from the media. It is through the media that they have a sense of the world beyond their immediate experience. The media inform public policy and influence public opinion, attitudes, behaviours and societal values. While media reports are socially constructed, people take them for reality and consider them to be normal, innocuous and natural. As Fleras (2003: 47) points out, the media "construct social realities by naturalizing our perceptions of the world as necessary and normal rather than conventional and created." It is also through the media that a vast majority of people develop their sense of ethnic, racial, gender and class identities. Henry and Tator (2002: 5) analogize that the media are like a mirror through which people see themselves; but the mirrors are often distorted as the media exaggerate the difference between ethnic groups and stereotype racially marginalized men and women. While the media's overt stereotyping and misrepresentation of racial minorities has declined over time, subtle images and sporadic negative coverage continue to marginalize and denigrate cultural and racial minorities (Fleras 2003). In recent Canadian history, overt misrepresentation and denigration of racial minorities has only receded but has not totally disappeared. There are case studies of blatant media representation of minorities involved in crime (Ma and Hildebrandt 1993; Creese and Peterson 1996; Tator and Henry 2006), in terrorism (Henry and Tator 2002) and in illegal migration (Hier and Greenberg 2002). Racialization in the media might go unnoticed because racist discourse can be couched in non-racist texts (Li 2001).

Anti-immigrant sentiments are now more contested by immigrants and public policy. Some media scholars have also claimed that the power elites no longer have the monopoly over the production of knowledge in the mainstream media because they have become the sites where the dominant ideology and discourse are countered and contested (Knight 1998a). In spite of the liberalization of the media space (McRobbie and Thornton 1995), the media continue to promote the reigning regimes of truth around race and ethnicity. Nevertheless, media misrepresentations of racial diversity are for the most part not deliberate. In the words of Fleras (2003: 283): "Media are racist in their coverage of minorities — not in deliberately disparaging minority women and men despite the prevalence of double standards and coded subtexts — but because of one-sided coverage that systematically denies, excludes, or marginalizes" (Fleras 2003: 283). What exists in Canada, according to Fleras (2003: 283), is "media racism." That is, racism exists in Canada's mainstream media, but racism is not their defining practice. Racism is only built into media structures. The problem of media misrepresentation may therefore be structural and institutional rather than personal or prejudicial (Fleras 2003: 284).

Mass Media and the Racialization of Infectious Diseases

The Othering of diseases is one of the many ways that the state regulates the conduct of its citizens, controls immigration and discourages prospective immigrants. As mentioned in the previous section, the Canadian press has participated in the racialization of various aspects of social life in Canada, but there has been very little scholarly study of the racialization of infectious diseases in the Canadian context. With the exception of Murdocca's (2003) analysis of media coverage of the non-Ebola case, there have been no comprehensive studies on media and the racialization of infectious diseases in Canada.[6] According to Murdocca (2003: 24), the Canadian press used the non-Ebola case to dichotomize the "racialized, diseased degenerate body" and the "respectable body" to reinforce a "national racial fantasy." Murdocca (2003: 24) demonstrates that racialization is a two-way process in the sense that defining the Other as the "degenerate body" automatically qualifies the Self as the "respectable body." She also asserts that the Othering process that the representation of the non-Ebola panic takes in the media served to justify the de-legitimization of the presence of non-Whites in Canadian society. In her words:

> The construction of the Canadian national story, then, has historically been interwoven with a colonial story of racial purity (white purity) and the absence of disease. The historical interdependency of racial purity and the absence of disease serves as just one example of the way in which racist ideologies of the innate degeneracy of "undesirable" populations served the purpose of carving out white supremacist ideals of national belonging. (Murdocca 2003: 26)

In addition to being racist, Murdocca (2003) claims that the coverage was sexist. Like Saartjie Baartman (a.k.a. Hottentot Venus), the patient became a medical curiosity and a spectacle for expressing Canadian nationalism. Saartjie Baartman was an African woman brought to England from South Africa by a Boer farmer in 1819. She was shown as an exhibit over five years in London and Paris (Hall 1997: 264). As a Black woman, she became a spectacle for the Europeans. Murdocca (2003) observes similarities between this historical event and the treatment of the patient in the media and by the medical establishment. She states that the "racialized spectacle can be thought of as a repackaged version of the Hottentot Venus who was precisely seen as a medical curiosity and utilized for the project of empire building" (Murdocca 2003: 30).

Historically, non-White women were ideologically and materially constructed as "outsiders" to the Canadian nation (see Thobani 2000). For example, Black women worked as domestics for White women and their families and were precluded by the Canadian state from becoming permanent residents and Canadian citizens (see Arat-Koc 2005). Conversely, European women were considered as the "mothers of the race" (Mawani 2002: 186). Thobani (2000: 287) argues that non-White women were defined as constituting a two-fold threat to the Canadian nation. First, the "presence" and "uncivilized practices" of non-White immigrant women in Canada "threatened to 'pollute the purity' of the Canadian nation"; and second, their capacity to reproduce future generations of non-White immigrants with legal and political claims to citizenship was a threat to the Whiteness of the Canadian nation. Dua's (2000) work on South Asian-Canadian women shows that racialized minority women in Canada are portrayed as the antithesis of mainstream Canadian women. Fleras and Kunz (2001: 115-117) point out that women are targets of media misrepresentation, but visible minority women also confront "miniaturized" representation and misrepresentation in the media because of their race. So, racialization interlocks with other systems of oppression, including gender (Jiwani 2006), but also immigration status, religion, ableism and sexual orientation (see Dua 2007). For example, women of colour are more prone to poverty, racism, deportation and violence than White women. Jiwani (2005: 50) notes that gender, race and nation converge in the formation of a unifying and homogeneous national identity. She claims that representations of women of colour in the popular media show that they are marginal to the nation (Jiwani 2005: 53). They are often constructed as

> pre-modern or anti-modernity, they are represented as symbolic victims of the cultures of Others — backward, barbaric, traditional, and oppressive.... As victims, they become recipients of Canadian benevolence signified through the various rescue attempts of the state and its agencies, and as survivors, they signify the success of multicultural tolerance and liberal values. (Jiwani 2005: 53)

The dearth of Canadian literature on the racialization of infectious diseases is compensated for by studies in other Western societies. A number of non-Canadian studies show how the media associate infectious diseases with the racial Other and shape public opinion and public policy around inter-racial relations. Power (1995) finds in his study of news media coverage of the bubonic plague in San Francisco in the 1900s that the etiology of the disease was attributed to the "Chinese Other," leading to further anti-Asian sentiments. Dubois (1996: 8) also points out that the American media participated in the blaming of Haitians for the emergence of AIDS:

> Many, including well-intentioned doctors and journalists, have participated in racist descriptions of the Haitian people and therefore in policies which have discriminated against them. In the early 1980s, the American media, following the lead of certain scientists, blamed Haitians as the source of a then new epidemic: AIDS. In doing so, they played into prevalent stereotypes about Haiti, deepening those stereotypes and magnifying the stigmatization they cause.

Deriving from a study by Ungar (1998), the Othering of a disease by the Western press reassures its audiences but also reinforces the notion of Western superiority in hygiene and medicine. Joffe and Haarhoff (2002) analyze the representations of mid-1990s Ebola outbreaks in parts of Africa in the British press and through interviews with newsreaders. They find that British broadsheets and tabloids Otherize Ebola by associating it with Africa and that the majority of their subscribers held similar views. The study suggests that there is a relationship between media discourse and public opinion. Washer's (2004) study of the representation of SARS in the British press highlights the association of SARS to the Chinese people's peculiar unsanitary lifestyle and their close proximity to animals. Washer (2004) maintains that the indigenization of the disease to China was reassuring to the British public, who had conceived the Chinese as the Other:

> The themes of difference, of dirt and "our" disgust at the way "they" live and what "they" eat begin to form into a coherent package. The (British) reader is led to place the responsibility for SARS at the feet of the Chinese and at the same time is reassured that "it couldn't happen here" because "we" don't live like that. (Washer 2004: 2568)

In both the non-Ebola and SARS cases, the African and the Chinese are constructed as the Other, which could only be rescued by Western science.

Methodology: Content Analysis and Interviews

Data for this book were derived from a content analysis of four major newspapers that covered the non-Ebola story and semi-structured interviews with four journalists,[7] two physicians, the director of media communications for

Henderson Incorporation in Hamilton and eighteen members of the Black community in Hamilton. The unrepresentative sample of the Black population in the study was divided into two categories for analytical convenience: nine were "Congolese Blacks" and nine were "non-Congolese Blacks." For the category "non-Congolese," their sub-ethnic affiliations were taken into consideration. Five were first generation immigrants from Africa; three were first generation immigrants from the Caribbean and one was Canadian-born whose genealogy in Canada dates back to the mid-nineteenth century's underground railway. Members of the Congolese community were selected because the Congolese did not have exactly the same experience and interpretation of the incident as the non-Congolese Blacks.[8]

The four Canadian newspapers examined were the *Toronto Star*, the *Hamilton Spectator*, the *National Post* and the *Globe and Mail*. These four Canadian newspapers were selected on the basis of their "ideological positions" and/or circulation. The *Toronto Star* caters to an economically and socially diverse group. In one study, it was argued that, "editorially," the *Toronto Star* is "a socially liberal paper" (Knight 2001: 77). The *Toronto Star* is a daily newspaper published in Toronto, but its audience is largely found in southern Ontario, and it has the largest circulation of any news daily in Canada (see Knight 2001: 77). The *Hamilton Spectator* is the local newspaper; it is published by the owner of the *Toronto Star* (Torstar) and similarly targets a diverse readership. It serves the local Hamilton community and neighbouring towns. Like the *Toronto Star*, the *Hamilton Spectator* is a daily newspaper. The *National Post* is a daily national newspaper that caters to the nation's intellectual and corporate elites, is generally considered a conservative press and is well known for its "anti-immigration perspective" (see Henry and Tator 2002: 111). Finally, the *Globe and Mail* is a daily newspaper that targets the interests of the economic and political elites. Though published in Toronto, it is a national newspaper that is editorially sympathetic to neo-liberal philosophy (Knight 2001: 77).

Opinion discourses and hard news spanning February 6 to March 14, 2001, form the basis of the newspaper analysis. Opinion discourses and hard news play equally significant roles in influencing the opinions of the news audience. In the case of hard news, it is considered to be fair, balanced and objective, whereas opinion discourses are considered as "overly biased viewpoints that are not intended to be objective, fair, or balanced" (Greenberg 2000: 3). Editorials are also opinionated; unlike hard news they are subjective. In spite of the differing qualities of opinion discourses and hard news, they both participate in recruiting the audience's association with preferred readings that serve the power elites (Hall et al. 1978).

The analysis of the newspaper coverage was comprised of two components. The first component was an analysis of key words used to qualify the Ebola disease in all headlines, captions and news stories. All news articles on

Ebola that appeared in the four newspapers were read to identify the dominant themes in the media narratives before they were coded. The frequency of words in the hard news was quantified to generate the major themes of the news coverage of the Ebola case. Major themes that emerged in the media narratives were coded as follows: panic; diseases; identity; suspicion/crime and immigration. These emerging themes form the substance of analysis (see appendix). Editorials and letters to the editor were not quantified for two reasons. First, unlike the hard news stories, editorials and letters to the editor lack the journalistic criterion of "objectivity." They represent what Fairclough (1998: 149) calls "the lifeworld discourse of ordinary people," that is, the shared world of everyday experience (see Fairclough 1998). Second, they were few in number: two editorials (one in the *Hamilton Spectator* and the other one in the *National Post*) and four letters to the editor (one in the *National Post*, two in the *Hamilton Spectator* and one in the *Toronto Star*). Nevertheless, they were set aside for the qualitative analysis of the study to elucidate the ideological influence of newspapers on their readership. Editorials are the "official voice of a media outlet on matters of public importance" (Greenberg 2000: 520). Letters to the editor are submitted by people not employed at a newspaper. They are written by ordinary citizens and are evaluated by a letters editor or other members of the editorial team for quality of writing, concision and in relation to all kinds of news values. The second component employs critical discourse analysis (van Dijk 1993a; Li 2001; Henry and Tator 2002) as a methodological approach unveiling the preferred meanings of a media content that appears neutral and innocuous. Unlike positivistic claims to neutrality in social science research, van Dijk (1993a) has claimed that critical discourse analysis does not deny the fact that the researcher occupies a subject location.[9]

Notes

1. Out of respect for the Congolese woman at the centre of this non-Ebola event, I refer to her throughout this book as "the patient" rather than by name.
2. As mentioned in the note in the Preface, this case is referred to as "non-Ebola," given that there was no actual incident of Ebola.
3. A few selected instances of racialization of immigration are provided here. For a full account of Canadian immigration and immigration policy since the mid-sixteenth century, read Knowles (1997).
4. While "peripheral Europeans" were largely disadvantaged in the past, they have, over time, overcome their social and economic inhibitions (Lian and Mathews 1998).
5. "Late modernity" is a term that describes contemporary modern societies (Giddens 1990, 1991; Hall 1992). This concept is discussed in depth in chapter 2.
6. Hier and Greenberg (2002: 503–505) describe how the media cross-articulate infectious diseases with "illegal" Fujianese migration to Canada for the purposes of causing a moral panic over the changing racial and cultural landscape of Canada through immigration. Their study is not a study of race and infectious diseases.

7. In the research design stage, eight journalists were to be interviewed for the study. Some of the journalists contacted declined an interview. The four that were interviewed for the study were very involved in the case.

8. The Congolese have a nuanced interpretation of the incident, which is well documented in chapter 5.

9. As a person of African descent, I concur with van Dijk's (2001) assertion that "theory formation, description, and explanation, also in discourse analysis, are sociopolitically 'situated,' whether we like it or not" (van Dijk 2001: 353).

Chapter 2

Media and Society

As in Isaac Newton's statement, "if I can see further, it is because I am standing on the shoulders of giants," this study relies largely on a set of variegated literature on the influence of the mass media on modern/late modern subjects. This chapter reviews the body of scholarly work on the ideological function of the media, the latent role of media texts on human behaviour and social relations and the role that human agency plays in people's appreciation of media discourse. Specifically, this chapter combines the literature on moral panic and the media, risk and collective behaviour, human agency and race and racialization.

Media and Ideology

The association of a disease with a racial Other in the media must commence with an examination of the role of the media in constituting what sociologist Max Weber (1968) refers to as *"Verstehen,"* or subjectivity. One major function of the mass media in modern societies is to inform the public. However, the information provided by the media is a construction of reality. Given that the mainstream media are owned and managed by people with status and power, van Dijk (1993a) notes that there is a relationship between the media and social inequality in modern societies. For example, those who own and control the media set the public policy agenda of society by using the media discourse to achieve Max Weber's notion of "legitimate domination" (Weber 1968).

Media scholars employ the concept of "ideology" to explain the legitimate domination of ordinary citizens by the few "power elites" of modern societies (Mills 1956). According to Althusser (1971), the media are a constituent of the "ideological state apparatus." The overarching definition of ideology in media studies is derived from the legacy of Marx. Fleras (2003: 49) defines ideology as a "set of ideas (about what is) and ideals (about what ought to be) that have the intent or effect of bolstering the prevailing distribution of power, wealth, and privilege." The effectiveness of ideologies lie in concealing contradictions in society by making the social appear natural and normal (Knight 1982). Given the important role that the media play as a key means for which subjects of modern societies derive knowledge about the world and their placement in it, the mainstream media are capable of systemically reproducing and reinforcing unequal relations (see Henry and

Tator 2002; Fleras 2003). With respect to ethno-racial relations, the media reinforce and maintain racial stratification by amplifying cultural differences between groups with myths and stereotypes.

Media discourses reflect and inflect the dominant ideologies (Hall 1977). News, for example, is ideological because real events are transformed into symbolic forms, as events on their own cannot signify and be made intelligible. The translation of real events into symbolic forms is referred to by Hall (1977, 1980) as "encoding." The process of encoding entails the selection of codes, assigning meanings to events and placing events in a referential context for the purpose of attributing meanings to them (Hall 1977: 343). The encoding of messages is an expression of dominant group's definitions of situations and events. Hall (1977) explains that encoding

> represents or refracts the existing structures of power, wealth and domination, hence that they *structure* every event they signify, and *accent* them in a manner which reproduces the given ideological structures — this process has become unconscious, even for the encoders. (Hall 1977: 344, emphasis original)

Hall also notes that the media are relatively autonomous of the state and members of its ruling cabals. The influence of the ruling elites is not often noticeable because it is insidious:

> For though the major political parties sharply disagree about this or that aspect of policy, there are fundamental agreements which bind the opposing positions into a complex unity: all the presuppositions, the limits to the argument, the terms of reference, etc., which those elements within the system must *share* in order to "disagree." It is this underlying "unity" which the media underwrite and reproduce: and it is in this sense that the ideological inflexion of media discourses are best understood, not as "partisan" but as fundamentally oriented "within the mode of reality of the state." (Hall 1977: 346, emphasis original)

Hall also states that the media reproduce society's patterns of unequal social relations through the ideology of the ruling class.

Knight (1982) posits that news is ideology because it is never impartial and represents the position of dominant members of society. He defines ideology as "a way of knowing and, obversely, not knowing about the world that is structured by broader relations of power and control" (Knight 1982: 17). Ideology works to make unequal social relations appear natural, making subjects concur with the dominant worldview. Knight (1982) provides three elements of journalistic practice that make news ideological. First, the news media rely heavily on official and expert sources, often representatives of powerful institutions, at the expense of alternative viewpoints of laypersons or ordinary members of society. Second, newsworthiness is driven by the criteria of "extraordinariness" and "controversy." The preoccupation with the controversial and extraordinary news ensures that events such as crime, scandal and strikes are given general coverage in the media. Whereas "there is an implicit topography of power in this pattern" (Knight 1982: 27) of selection, most often "the activities of economic elites, for example, are relatively immune to journalistic inquiry by virtue of the privacy accorded to private property" (Knight 1982: 27). Therefore, what constitutes bad news is discerned by the definition proffered by the dominant ideology based on the discretion and norms of the dominant class.

The third element of journalistic practice that makes news ideological is the journalistic notion of "empiricism": the separation of "fact" from "opinion." Empiricism plays a major role in the ideological construction of news in two ways. First, since news places emphasis on "immediacy" and "actuality," it can then play down the "question of historical connectedness and development" (Knight 1982: 31). Second, "immediacy" connotes "directness of communication in which actuality is conveyed in uncontaminated, pristine form from actor to reader" (Knight 1982: 31). Therefore, news becomes represented and taken as original, undiluted, and not an abstraction of what actually took place. On the basis of these three elements involved in the production of news, Knight concludes that news is selective and occlusive (Knight 1982: 33). Selection "takes place in accordance with norms that are so deeply embedded in the practical routines of professional journalism that they are largely taken-for-granted by the practitioners themselves" (Knight 1982: 33). The partial accounts of news is an indication of its "occlusiveness," in the sense that other possible representations of events go unreported.

Although the news, Knight (1982) claims, refracts the perspectives of the middle class and above to the exclusion of those of the classes below, news production is neither "conspiratorial" nor an "ideological dupe" for class dominance. This is the reason why Knight states that "biased news stories" are "part of a more fundamental process of cultural stratification and exclusion which operates not at the level of more or less conscious conspiracies, but at a far deeper level of taken-for-grantedness" (Knight 1982: 21). Hall's (1981) position is consistent with this assertion, when he states that the media function is "the result of a set of complex, often contradictory, social relations; not the personal inclinations of its members" (Hall 1981: 20). For this reason, it is simplistic to declare that news, as ideology, is passively received by the audience.

Hall (1980) identifies the limitations of the linear model of news readers as passive, affirming that there are no deterministic relationships between the "encoding" and "decoding" of media contents. Put differently, there is no necessary correspondence between meanings encoded in a message and the unpacking or interpretation of the message. Hall (1980) identifies three ways that an encoded script can be decoded. First is the "dominant-hegemonic position," entailing acceptance of the dominant definition of a message by the audience. As Hall (1980: 136) explains, the "viewer is operating inside the dominant code." The second form that encoding can take is the "negoti-ated code or position" (Hall 1980: 137). Decoding within this version means adopting the dominant-hegemonic frame "while reserving the right to make a more negotiated application to 'local condition'" (Hall 1980: 137). Lastly, messages can be decoded in "a globally contrary way." Put differently, the audience operates with an "oppositional code" (Hall 1980: 138). This entails an oppositional reading to the preferred code. Concerning the third type, audiences interpret what they see in the media in terms of their past experi-ences and in terms of attitudes they have already developed (see chapters 4 and 5). What this implies is that there is no singular audience but multiple audiences and interpretations. According to Knight (1982), it is the possibil-ity of the readers of news to read different meanings from news items that makes news ideological. This means that

> the reader is not simply a "consumer" of predetermined content, but rather an active agent, an accomplice of ideology… it is precisely because of the requirement and allowance of subjectivity that ideol-ogy can deny itself as a relation of domination, and portray itself as "merely" a system of "value" and "belief." (Knight 1982: 36)

Seale (2002: 31) claims that there is a relationship between the audience making sense of media content and what he calls a "jointly shared stock of common knowledge." In his words:

> Readers are being invited to share in discursively producing a ver-sion of the world. The life of the media text depends on pre-existing frames, templates, stereotypes or common constructions between producers and audiences, which involve a process of active construc-tion of meaning by audiences, though usually within the confines of dominant scripts. (Seale 2002: 31)

Hay (1996) further argues against the structuralist Marxist notion of ideology as "interpellating" or "hailing" its subjects by "impairing" their judgment and making them unconsciously reproduce the dominant ideol-ogy (Althusser 1971; also see Horkheimer and Adorno 1982). Hay (1996) notes that subjects are not ideological dupes because they take part in the process of their hailing or interpellation. Hay shows that media texts invite readers and decoders to identify with a particular "preferred" subject position: as victims, heroes, heroines, underdogs, racial minorities or women. Also, readers of news may resist their interpellation by failing to recognize their hailing, by assuming the subject position of the Other or by outrightly rejecting the plot construction of the news (Hay 1996: 262–64). The reception of media is mediated by individuals' lived experience; therefore subjects' social location would influence the direction of their identification with media texts. Hay (1996) identifies two modes of interpellation, that is, two ways that a reader can identify with a subject position. First, individuals can identify individuated or direct modes of interpellation in the way that they are invited to recognize themselves in the news story. For example, news narratives can associate the audience or the public with a national crisis by using words like "we," "our" or "us." These are words that speak to people directly (see chapter 3). Second, individuals can identify through "empathic modes of interpellation" (Hay 1996: 263). Individuals are called or recruited to "empathize with, and thereby temporarily inhabit, the subject position of a victim whose experience we are unlikely directly to share" (Hay 1996: 263). Hay adds that an empathic mode of interpellation is a form of construction that counterpoises "an evil 'other' with an idealized innocent victim, into whose subject position we are interpellated" (Hay 1996: 263).

Framing and Ideology

"Framing" and "ideology" are two complementary concepts in media analysis. Drawing on the concept of framing, Knight (2001) and Entman (1993) assert that the news media select and partially represent "reality." Framing therefore entails discerning what is to be excluded, included or inserted in the news. Included items are often the ones that are congruent with the agenda of the news media and their ideological frames. Altheide (2002) refers to framing as "a parameter or boundary, for discussing a particular event" (Altheide 2002: 45). Specifically, frames "focus on what will be discussed, how it will be discussed, and, above all, how it will not be discussed" (Altheide 2002: 45). The choice of themes, therefore, requires that themes are organized in order of priorities, or what Astroff and Nyberg (1992) refer to as a "hierarchy of discourses." Framing often leads to the suppression of alternative and ordinary voices (Knight 1998b). Ordinary voices as the voices of opposition get less attention in the media not only because they are considered non-credible but also because of their weak ties with powerful institutions. The dominant or official perspective is usually placed on a higher level of credibility than alternative ones, which are more organized than the ordinary voice. For this reason, Hall et al. (1978) claim that the mass media reproduce power inequalities in such a way that unequal power relations become routinized and taken for granted:

Many of these structured forms of communication are so common, so natural, so taken for granted, so deeply embedded in the very communication forms which are employed, that they are hardly visible at all, as ideological constructs, unless we deliberately set out to ask, "What, other than what has been said about this topic, could be said?" "What questions are omitted?" "Why do the questions — which always presuppose answers of a particular kind — so often recur in this form? Why do certain other questions never appear?" (Hall et al. 1978: 65)

Framing plays a major role in media "agenda setting." To set an agenda is to focus on certain events and ignore other ones. Knight (1998b: 120) posits that "the process of agenda setting also occurs within as well as between topics, as the media distinguish and evaluate aspects of a particular event or issue." Rowe (1984) shows that items that are selected by the media qualify for "news values." The criteria for news values, according to Knight (1998b), are "extraordinariness," "personalization" and "immediacy" (see Knight 1998b: 112). Using the terms of reference set by three anti-immigration programs in Australia as an example, Rowe (1984) points out that there is a relationship among agenda setting, news values and ideology. The process of selecting newsworthy items entails exclusion of others. Exclusion of some items entails inclusion of others. This process is informed by ideology or a particular way of viewing the world. The media set an agenda when they are "able to tell people not only *what* to think about, but also *how* to think about it" (Knight 1998b: 120, emphasis original). To this end, Rowe (1984: 18) states that "the requirements of gaining and holding attention lead frequently to simplification, exaggeration, selective presentation, etc., in the production of a clear and coherent 'angle.'"

Mass Media, Moral Panic and Collective Behaviour

The literature on moral panic has provided insights into the relationship between the mass media and collective social action (Cohen 1972; Hall et al. 1978; Critcher 2003). Hall et al (1978) ground their analyses of moral panics in episodic reaction to social and economic change and argue that moral panic discourse provides a rallying point for the power elites to seek hegemony in times of social change. Drawing on the Gramscian strain of Marxism, Hall et al. argue that the media helped the British ruling class amplify a crisis in order to cement its hegemony at a time of fragile consensus in Britain. Through what Hall et al. refer to as a "signification spiral," urban Black youth, who were constructed as the "folk devil," were criminalized in their entirety. The disproportional reaction to the objective harm of crime associated with the urban youth was motivated by the signification spiral — "a way of signifying events which also intrinsically escalates their threat" (Hall et al. 1978: 223). One of the escalating mechanisms of the signification spiral is "convergence," which entails a cross articulation of two or more events "so as to implicitly or explicitly draw parallels between them" (Hall et al. 1978: 223). Articulations of diseases with the racialized Other (see Austin 1990; Tomes 2000; Chirimuuta and Chirimuuta 1989; Power 1995; Dubois 1996; Washer 2004) and sexual minorities (see Thompson 1998) have been empirically grounded in recent studies.

Goode and Ben-Yehuda (1994: 135) refer to Hall et al.'s perspectives on moral panics as "an elite-engineered model": "a conscious undertaking by the elite group to generate and sustain concern, fear, and panic on the part of the public over an issue that they recognize not to be terribly harmful to the society as a whole." In lieu of this perspective (the elite-engineered model), Goode and Ben-Yehuda (1994) favour an articulation of what they refer to as "grassroots model" and "interest group theory." They argue that moral panic is not an ideological imposition from the top, given that the situation leading to a moral panic must be organic to a society. Thus, a grassroots model of moral panic posits that "panics originate with the general public; the concern about a particular threat is a widespread, genuinely felt — if perhaps mistaken — concern" (1994: 127). However, public concerns do not lead into a panic unless they are articulated. Therefore, Goode and Ben-Yehuda state that moral panics stem from the middle rungs of society. Interest groups, they claim, such as "professional associations, police departments, the media, religious groups [and] educational organizations" have the ability to shape "the content or timing of panics" (1994:139).

Scholars like Goode and Ben-Yehuda maintain that a moral panic flounders in the absence of a grassroots endorsement, because pre-existing fears and concerns need to be brought to public attention by those in the middle rungs of society. In this view, the media cannot be held fully responsible for fuelling panics given that there must be prevailing issues or sentiments for the media to tap into. Thus, Goode and Ben-Yehuda's approach to the concept of moral panic has an influence on the current study of the non-Ebola panic. While the power elite plays a major role in using the media to influence the public, apropos Hall et al. (1978), the public only responds positively to the elite's discourse of domination in situations where the discourse resonates with their material condition and understanding of the world (Hier 2002b).

Globalization, Risks and Anti-Racial-Diversity Sentiments

The works of Giddens (1990, 1991) and Beck (1992) emphasize the existential peril of contemporary living. While conflicts over the distribution of material resources characterized the early stage of modernity, risk becomes an organizing principle of the second phase of modernity. Giddens (1990, 1991) refers to the second phase of modernity as "late modernity." Late modernity is a radicalized form of modernity, characterized by reflexivity and accelerated change involving the erosion of the categorical identity of class that was the master narrative of early modernity (Hall 1992: 280).

Risks of late modernity include environmental risks, such as pollution, floods and fire and also medical risks, such as improper medical care and treatment and deadly infectious diseases (see Lupton 1999). The preponderance of risks in the contemporary world leads to social anxiety. In the words of Beck:

> The driving force in the class society can be summarized in the phrase: *I am hungry!* The movement set in motion by the risk society, on the other hand, is expressed in the statement: *I am afraid! The commonality of anxiety* takes the place of the commonality of need. The type of the risk society marks in this sense a social epoch in which solidarity from anxiety arises and becomes a political force. (1992: 49, emphasis original)

Time-space compression is also one of the features of globalization (Hall 1992: 300). The sequestration of time from space (Giddens 1990, 1991) and time-space compression by telecommunications and improved transportation (Hall 1992: 300) globalize risks. For example, infectious diseases like Ebola and SARS that emerged in rural parts of the world can impose a sense of disorder on populations of urban centres of "global cities" (see Ali and Keil 2006). Giddens (1990, 1991) claims that "time-space distanciation" radicalizes modernity and connects us "with events, with actions, and with the visible appearance of physical settings thousands of miles away from where we happen to live" (Giddens 1990: 141). The separation of time from space, therefore, necessitates the "intrusion of distant events into everyday consciousness" (Giddens 1991: 27). Through the separation of time from space, health and other risks become unbounded, de-localized and globally threatening. Giddens' (1990) notion of time-space distanciation to describe globalization sounds jargonistic, but becomes interesting when tested empirically. Joffe and Haarhoff's (2002) study of Ebola in the British press is an affirmation of Giddens' notion of time-space distanciation, showing that lay persons gain their knowledge of "far-flung diseases" like Ebola through the mass media.

Major modern risks are human-made and are often consequences of globalization (Beck 1992). Lupton and Tulloch (2001: 20) describe such examples of these risks as "the dangers associated with nuclear weapons, the threat of ecological catastrophe, the collapse of global economic systems and *the rapid spread of new viruses across the world via travel*" (emphasis added). Giddens (1991, 1990) illustrates that risks are a condition of human life.

Humans only survive in the midst of risks because of the immunity they have developed from infancy. Giddens (1991) notes that human beings have always developed fortitude to cope with risks and their attendant existential insecurity through the security system they develop. Early in the life of a human, the infant forges relationships with caretakers through habit and routine. The relationships are based on basic trust. Basic trust links the Self to the object world and others, even in their absence. Everyday routines and habits provide immunity against threatening anxieties, without which a person would be easily overwhelmed by "ontological insecurity" (Giddens 1991: 39).

The routines instilled in the infant, and the trust it vested in its caretakers, provide the infant with "ontological security," a form of "emotional inoculation against existential anxieties — protection against future threats and dangers which allows the individual to sustain hope and courage in the face of whatever debilitating circumstances she or he might later confront" (Giddens 1991: 39). Basic trust is an emotional defensive mechanism, which is a "defensive carapace or protective cocoon which all normal individuals carry around with them as the means whereby they are able to get on with the affairs of day-to-day life" (Giddens 1991: 40). If it were not for the basic trust, everyone would be prone to anxieties about risks:

> The sustaining of life, in a bodily sense as well as in the sense of psychological health, is inherently subject to risk. The fact that the behavior of human beings is so strongly influenced by mediated experience, together with the cumulative capacities which human agents possess, means that every human individual could (in principle) be overwhelmed by anxieties about risks which are implied by the very business of living. That sense of "invulnerability" which blocks off negative possibilities in favor of a generalized attitude of hope derives from basic trust. (Giddens 1991: 40)

However, the "protective cocoon" that allows people to carry on with their daily activities in the presence of risks is a sense of "unreality" rather than "a firm conviction of security," as the "protective barrier it offers may be pierced, temporarily or more permanently, by happenings which demonstrate as real the negative contingencies built into all risk" (Giddens 1991: 40). People can be overwhelmed by anxiety when their routines of life are disrupted. Richmond (1994) makes a distinction between primary and secondary ontological insecurities. The former is derived from a "collapse of the normal routines of daily life." Whereas, security is contingent on "the predictability and reliability of key political, economic, and social institutions" (Richmond 1994: 19), secondary ontological insecurity is experienced "when particular spheres of social life are threatened. When political systems degenerate into anarchy and civil war, or revolutions overthrow established forms of government, security is threatened" (Richmond 1994: 19). Richmond's insight into social anxiety also affirms the vulnerability of human beings to insecurity in the face of social change. In a media-saturated world, health risks, for example, do not have to be experienced directly before a sense of unreality is interrupted and the protective barrier that Giddens mentions is shattered. Insecurity is more pronounced in contemporary Western societies by the metastructural change that institutions and individuals have been undergoing since the second half of the twentieth century. For example, the Internet and globalization have exposed humans to events and activities beyond their immediate environment, making them capable of reflecting on things like global economic changes and health threats because they have profound effects on everyone (Ritzer 2007: 61).

Stuart Hall (1992: 275) characterized the late modern condition as the loss of a "social sense of self." Ontological insecurity is a corollary of people's obsession with the Self in contemporary societies. The de-centring of Self accords human freedom, but limitless self-determination is fraught with difficulties and tensions (see Ritzer 2007: 61). Previously, people paid less attention to who they were because they were too preoccupied with survival and material wants, but today the Self is subject to constant scrutiny (Ritzer 2007: 61). Ritzer applies this idea to Giddens' claim that the Self (i.e., self-awareness or self-reflection) is no longer *a* project but *the* project for many people in contemporary Western societies.

The notion of ontological insecurity translates into what Barrett (1994: 269) refers to as "pan-human insecurity." Barrett's (1994) conceptual framework helps to explain the nature of ethno-racial relations when society undergoes social change. He claims that while pan-human insecurity is one of the pre-conditions of racism, it does not inevitably lead to it. Barrett (1994) further argues that there are social structural determinants of racism, among which are colonialism, nationalism and media portrayal of minorities. In other words, the factors of media portrayals of minorities, nationalism and colonialism significantly intensify racism. However, the specific triggering factors of racism pertain to immediate social events such as downward swings in the economy, changes in immigration patterns and celebrated incidents of minority persecution. During the time of the non-Ebola scare, Canada was experiencing what Barrett (1994: 270) described as "changes in immigration patterns" and "celebrated incidents of minority persecution" (see Hier and Greenberg 2002 for a recent incidence of this).

Over the past three decades, but much more so since the 1990s, there have been concerns in the Canadian public over the sustenance of the "Canadian national identity" in the face of globalization (see Simmons 1998b; Zong 1997). With reference to racial diversity, globalization and changes in immigration patterns that Barrett (1994) mentions, Li (2003) shows that anxieties have risen in Canada in the past few years over the presence of non-European immigrants — Asians, Africans and "visible minorities" — who are distinguished by their somatic differences from Whites

The concerns of Canadians over immigration from non-traditional sources are documented in Barrett's ethnographic study of ethno-racial relations in a rural Ontario community undergoing social and economic change, including increasing racial diversity. The following are some of the accounts in Barrett's (1994) ethnographic study:

> A few weeks before I met her, she had taken a trip to Toronto: "I kept thinking, where are the white people? I felt like a foreigner in my own country." She was particularly displeased about the number of Asian-origin people she had seen: "I have something about Pakistanis. I'm getting a little pissed off about the ones wearing turbans; you know, in the Mounties, and the daggers." (Barrett 1994: 249)

> He insisted that he himself had no respect for racists, but added: "I realize what you call the old English descent is going to be extinct. We're letting too many coloreds in. They'll soon tell *us* what to do!" (Barrett 1994: 249)

> Third world immigrants were a different matter. He thought that they should not be allowed to speak their own languages in public, and he accused the government of providing them with jobs while "Canadians" starved. Like others, he opposed any concessions to visible minorities in organizations such as the RCMP: "I'm totally against Mounties wearing turbans. I'm pro-Canada. I don't like to see Canada broken down into cultures." (Barrett 1994: 251)

What the ideas of Li (2003) and Barrett (1994) show is that, like in European countries, especially the Netherlands, Britain, Germany (see Husbands 1994) and Austria (see Wodak and Matouschek 1993), social change involving ethnic or racial diversity correlates highly with anti-racial-diversity sentiments in Canada. Li (2001, 2003) points out that such attitudes in the Canadian public are rooted in racism and racialization. These studies and others on racial conflict show that it is a pan-human psychological desire to excise the Other in times of sweeping societal change. It is always the case that people deal with anxiety by deflecting it into other realms:

> The creative and imaginative forms which defenses against anxiety take can explain the fact that the subject is not simply a product of the social environment. Whatever is repressed because it is threat-

ening to the integrity of the self (thereby provoking anxiety) does not disappear, but manifests in indirect ways; for example through displacement onto another arena in a person's life or indeed onto another person or idea or group. (Hollway and Jefferson 1997: 262)

The construction of the racial/ethnic Other as "enemy stereotypes" in times of uncertainty and insecurity can provide certitude for a population under stress (see Hier 2003). The media construction of the Other can tap into (pre) existing conditions. The Other tends to be easily constructed where there are gross inequalities of power (Hall 1997, 1981).

Representations of Blacks in the Media

In both literary (Achebe 1989) and media texts (Brookes 1995), Africans are represented as indubitably different from Europeans (Achebe 1989; Razack 2004). In Western media, Africans are visually and verbally represented as the Other. In her analysis of the Canadian military's documentary, *Witness the Evil*, and the CBC's *Unseen Scars*, on post-traumatic stress disorder (PTSD) suffered by peacekeepers, Razack (2004) notes that Africans are represented in these documentaries as the epitomes of evil. According to her, Africa and Africans exist in the Western mind as backward and barbaric, and so need Western peacekeepers to expurgate them of their evil. In Razack's (2004: 20) words: "images of mutilated bodies, fields filled with corpses, and large piles of machetes dramatically convey a brutality that is frequently described as an apocalypse." In these documentaries, Razack (2004) observes that Africans lack subjectivity and agency, and notes that denigrating representations of Africa and Africans can only make sense to Western subjects through the idiom of race.

Achebe (1989) claims that the portrayal of the peoples of the Congo in Conrad's *Heart of Darkness* (1950) stemmed from the pre-existing image of Africa in nineteenth-century Europe. Nevertheless, the portrayal of Africans and Africa in the book is considered by Achebe as dehumanizing and as continuing to foster age-long racist attitudes towards Africa in the world. Achebe argues that Africans and Africa exist in the Western imagination as an antithesis. He states, thus: "it is the desire... in Western psychology to set Africa up as a foil to Europe, as a place of negations at once remote and vaguely familiar, in comparison with which Europe's own state of spiritual grace will manifest" (Achebe 1989: 2–3). In a similar vein, Sanders (2005) states in his analysis of the media and police reaction to the discovery of a boy's torso in the River Thames in England that Africans and the African diaspora in the U.K. were represented "as people who hold weird, inexplicable, and morally bankrupt beliefs" (Sanders 2005: 132). He notes that contemporary representations of Africa in the Western media and the general perceptions of Africa by the Europeans are rooted in history. He states that derogatory imagery of Africa that exists in the West draws "on a lengthy Western history of demonizing Others and are refracted through specific contemporary constellations of power" (Sanders 2005: 136).

Brookes (1995) has claimed that naturalized assumptions of negativity about Africa exists within Western epistemologies, and those assumptions are the products of the colonial discourse. Discourses, as Hall (1992: 314) explains, do not stop abruptly: "They go unfolding changing shape, as they make sense of new circumstances. They often carry many of the same unconscious premises and unexamined assumptions in their blood stream." Brookes (1995) posits that there are traces of old racist stereotypes in the contemporary image of Africa in the media:

> The historical discourses of travelers, missionaries, anthropologists, biologists and colonialists on African primitiveness, savagery, the hierarchy of civilizations, the evolution of the species and accompanying notions of European racial superiority show remarkable ideological similarity to current discourse on Africa, suggesting a significant influence and homogenizing effect on current discourse. (Brookes 1995: 487)

Hall (1997) identifies the root of the contemporary negative representation of Blacks in the media. He argues that the representation of Blacks and Africans in Western media is a reflection of the historical asymmetries between the "West" and the "Rest." Hall (1997) identifies three historical moments that deeply damaged the image of Africa and people of African descent, and have shaped the contemporary image of Africans and Blacks as a racial Other: first, the early encounters of West African kingdoms and European traders in the sixteenth century, which resulted in the cartel slave trade for three hundred years; second, the era of colonialism and imperialism, when Africa was partitioned by the major European powers; and third, the period following Second World War migrations from the economic periphery of the world to North America and Europe (Hall 1997: 239).

Agency and Contested Hegemonies

Knight (1998a), in his analysis of the New Right commonsense revolution in Ontario in the 1990s, finds constant struggles among three kinds of news sources: official, ordinary and alternative sources. Through the ordinary and alternative sources, victims of the New Right politics articulate their plight and apportion blame to the powerful, the government and its policies. The alternative source, Knight (1998a) argues, can activate local anti-government protests by fusing the "feeling passion" of ordinary people with their external material understanding of situations (common sense). Thus, the political economy of power became counterpoised to the "moral economy of harm" as the media also granted ordinary and alternative sources some attention. The harm and pain of the New Right politics, Knight claims, generates a "feeling passion" — the fusion of knowledge and understanding with the lived experiential consciousness of the world in ways that are normatively and emotionally resonant — in the audiences. Knight (1998a: 122) explains:

> This fusion can compromise or undermine the advantage that formal inequalities of power give to official sources and the institutions and organizations they represent… it is common for the media to use the passive voice to represent events and issues, and this is usually the case where actions of those with status and authority have adverse consequences for others… the obverse effect of the passive voice, however, is to transform the objects of real world actions, the victims of authority, into the subjects of representation. This inversion can lead to the foregrounding of their situation and experiences, their feelings and reactions, in a personalized, emotional, and normatively invested way that has critical implications for the exercise of power.

Knight (1998a) concludes that the dominant group, or those in power, do not occupy an unchallenged position in the media space because there are available avenues or opportunities for the political economy of power to be "confronted openly by the moral economy of harm in which ordinary victims, and their supporters and representatives, enjoy a degree of discursive influence over the grounds on which hegemony is contested and negotiated" (Knight 1998a: 124).

McRobbie's (1994) observation is similar to that of Knight. Compared to the past, McRobbie posits that "folk devils" are now more difficult to create explicitly because of the expanded scale of the media and relative cheapness and ease of access to them, which have allowed folk devils the opportunity to "fight back." In the case of racialized groups, they are not often passive in the face of domination; they react to their subordination by inverting their racial categorization and using it as a valour. The use of race/ethnicity as a resource for mobilization (see Olzak 1983; Akioye 1994; Adeyanju 2003) is a result of "other-definition" or racial categorization that inadvertently leads to "self-definition" by racialized groups. This explains why Satzewich (1998b: 33–34) and Miles (1989: 72) state that racial categorization is not necessarily devalourizing, as racialized groups can seize on it to resist their oppression. Consider Miles' (1989: 72–73) point:

> Certain somatic characteristics (usually skin color) have been sig-nified as the foundation for a common experience and fate as an

excluded population, irrespective of class position and cultural origin, as a result of which a political appeal to "race" (commonly in the form of an appeal to "blackness") is made in order to effect a political mobilization intended to reverse material and political disadvantage as well as colonial rule.

It can be inferred that the preponderance of media and their disparate perspectives has made it possible for relatively powerless groups to articulate their issues and contest their (mis)representation in the media. Nevertheless, further studies need to be conducted to ensure that the opportunities available for minorities are not being exaggerated. Social variables such as culture, class and status may still mediate the quality of resistance and challenge to dominant discourses in the media. In the case study of Hier (2002a), for example, members of the rave community contest the discursive construction of rave culture as a potential serious health risk to them and the public at large, averting a maturation of the risk of rave into a full blown moral panic. Hier (2002a) fails to indicate the extent to which the youth's cultural capital supports their claims made via the media. Wilson and Atkinson's (2005) study of offline and online activities of ravers and straightedge youth suffers the same oversight. In ethnically diverse and immigrant-receiving countries, new immigrants may arrive in their new society with an incongruent cultural capital and other factors that can constrain them from re-defining themselves in the media in instances where they are misrepresented. As chapter 4 discusses, the views of members of the Congolese community were discredited by journalists and the media because of their weak attachment to major Canadian social institutions.

News as a social construction is an overarching theme of this chapter. For social constructionists, meanings are not inherent but attributed to things by people. Thus, "news is a social convention constructed by individuals who make choices about what stories to tell and how to tell them, albeit within broader and constraining contexts" (Fleras 2003: 119). But news matters because people use it to understand their worlds. This chapter has illustrated that the news media produce knowledge in a certain way that influences and organizes everyday life. Henry and Tator (2002: 5) equate the media to a mirror, something like the "looking glass self" of Cooley (1962). However, Henry and Tator (2002: 5) claim that the image that the mirror produces is distorted because news media produce information that bolsters the interests of the elites and perpetuates the status quo. Given the central role that the media play in modern life, they are capable of amplifying contemporary risks across time and space. They can also cross-articulate those contemporary risks with ethno-racial differences and problematize racial diversity.

The media audience is not a passive recipient of media discourse.

While the media tap into the consumers' experiential consciousness of the material world, the consumers participate in their own recruitment into the media discourse. Miles and Brown (2003: 106) argue that people draw on their material understanding of the world or *Erlebnis* before they accept or reject the dominant ideology. In the case of media representation of racial diversity, the articulation of historical discourses of the racial Other with contemporary ones can recruit the commonsense of the public or resonate with what Gramsci refers to as "feeling passion": the point where individuals' understandings of how the social world "is" intersects with their lived experiences as to fuse a perception or understanding of reality with lived experience in a manner which is emotionally and normatively resonant (Hier 2002b: 318). In the end, the media articulation of immigration from non-conventional regions of the world with diseases is capable of fusing the feeling passion of ordinary people with their material understanding of situations (see Knight 1998a). Part of the reviewed literature in this chapter is directly applicable to the non-Ebola panic, especially the segments on moral panic and collective behaviour, globalization and risk, and agency and counter-hegemony. Other parts are not directly applied because they hold certain assumptions that are unconfirmed in many studies that adopt content analysis. As is pointed out in the next chapter, content analysis of newspapers does not offer a convincing explanation of how people actually respond to media items. In this particular study there is no evidence to show that it was the media that recruited, with their anti-immigration rhetoric, White Canadians against immigration. The testimonials of members of the Black community in chapters 4 and 5 about their experiences during the coverage and after do not say much about the effects of the coverage on the Canadian public. Interviewing Canadians who gained their understanding of the non-Ebola case in Canada would have provided information about the relationship between [White] audience attitude and the news reports.[1] Nevertheless, the reviewed literature shows that media matters cannot be taken with levity because of the media's capacity to provide their consumers with information that is already ideologically inflected.

Note

1. Studies by Joffe and Haarhoff (2002) and Kitzinger (1998a, 1998b) involved interviews with consumers of news events relating to race/ethnicity and infectious diseases.

Chapter 3

The Media Discourse of Race, Immigration and Health Risks

The mass media have the capability to present information about events that occur outside of the immediate and direct experience of the majority of society (Hall et al. 1978). In considering the central importance of the mass media to the structure of society, van Dijk (1993a) asserts that the media are an important vehicle through which an ensemble of dominant ideas in society is disseminated to its members. News reporters and journalists are considered front line workers in the case of representing and telling the stories of the greater world beyond the reach of the ordinary citizen. Although modern journalism is a profession that makes claim to "value neutrality" and "objectivity" in the reporting of stories (Knight 1982: 18), it often misrepresents racial minorities and reinforces existing social inequalities in society (van Dijk 1991, 1993a; Fleras 1994; Henry and Tator 2002).[1]

This chapter examines the Canadian press coverage of the non-Ebola panic.[2] The Canadian press used the non-Ebola case to problematize the immigration of non-Europeans to Canada by its cross-articulation with racial diversity and health risks to Canadians. As well, this chapter illustrates how the notion of "race" can be sustained in non-racial terms (see Barker 1981; Henry and Tator 2006; Li 2001). Beck (1992) has indicated that risk consciousness in a risk society is not only rampant but that conflicts over risk get displaced. The displacement model of risk leads Beck to suggest that the risk society is a "scapegoat society" (Beck 1992:75). The anti-racial-diversity subtexts in the print media, as it is argued in this chapter, serve as an index of the collective insecurities of Canadians stemming from the "disorder" of social change. The anxiety over these insecurities is displaced to non-European immigrants in an attempt to impose a sense of social order (see Barrett 1994; Li 2003). It is therefore contended that the media reports on the suspected Ebola case, contextualized as a problem of immigration, find resonance in a public that already has what Barrett (1994: 270) refers to as "racial capacity," largely derived from the colonial discourse on the Other. It is thus argued that when racist discourses are articulated in *non-racist terms* via media coverage, members of the public are actively and emotively involved in the interpretation of what they see in the media in terms of their past experiences and in relation to attitudes they have developed through the "mutual knowledge incorporated in encounters" (Giddens 1984: 4).

Sections one, two, three and four of the chapter focus on the themes of panic, identity and immigration and their articulation with health risks and crime respectively. The final section combines hard news with letters to the editor and editorials to show the salience of anti-racial-diversity subtexts in the coverage and their (re)presentation in a race-neutral way.

Panic

A key theme in the media coverage of the non-Ebola case is panic. Panics are conveyed in the choice of words in headlines and in the body of news articles.

Headlines

According to van Dijk (1991), headlines have both cognitive and textual functions (van Dijk 1991: 50). Most readers do not read the remainder of an article, taking with them the summarized version of the news in the headline. While there is no indication in the early coverage that the hospital had diagnosed Ebola, the word was already embedded in some of the news headlines. Meningitis, malaria and a broad category of hemorrhagic fevers, including Marburg and Crimean-Congo, are other possible infections displaying similar symptoms to Ebola. Despite these possibilities, however, "Ebola" is the choice word for the headlines. It constitutes 40 percent of key words in headlines of the *National Post*, about 17 percent of those found in the *Hamilton Spectator*, 55.6 percent of the *Globe and Mail*'s and 33.3 percent of those of the *Toronto Star* at the early stage when Ebola was suspected (see appendix). The following are some examples of the newspaper headlines with the word "Ebola":

> Mystery virus fells woman, Ebola not ruled out, Woman arrived from the Congo (*Hamilton Spectator* February 6, 2001)

> Doctors fear woman may have Ebola (*Toronto Star* February 6, 2001)

> Ebola fever case feared, Woman from Congo in Hamilton (*Globe and Mail* February 6, 2001)

Ebola remains a key word in the newspaper headlines after February 8, 2001, even when it was already ruled out by medical tests. Just over 30 percent of the key words in the *Toronto Star* contain "Ebola," 18.2 percent for the *Globe and Mail*, 39.3 percent for the *Hamilton Spectator*, and close to 32 percent for the *National Post* in their post-Ebola coverage.

Apart from the use of the word "Ebola," another notable "panicky" word is "mystery." Giddens (1991) reminds us of the distinction between anxiety and fear: "fear is a response to a specific threat and therefore has a definite object" (Giddens 1991: 43), whereas "anxiety is diffuse, it is free floating: lacking a specific object" (Giddens 1991: 44). While "Ebola" signifies a detectable fear, "mystery" relates to anxiety — an unknown enemy, with no cure, which strikes without warning. Therefore, anxiety may evoke feelings of uncertainty and insecurity and the sense that "it could happen to you"[3] (Wardle 2006: 517). The following are some examples:

> Mystery illness strikes woman (*Toronto Star* February 6, 2001)

> Disease mystery unsolved, Doctors are still bewildered by Congolese woman's illness (*Hamilton Spectator* February 10, 2001)

> Woman with mystery illness on life-support, Condition worsens (*National Post* February 9, 2001)

Here agency is given to a virus: it can "strike." When the media gave the "mystery illness" agency, it may be comprehended by the public as capable of invasion (see Gwyn 1999), that is, programmed to harm.

The emphasis on "woman" in the headlines is a reminder of the racialized female body that Hall (1997) describes as characterizing the "spectacle of the other," and that which Lavani (1995) classifies as exotic and dangerous in colonial discourse. In the Orientalist version of colonial discourse to which Lavani (1995) alludes, women were constructed as the Other racially and sexually. As the Other, women constitute danger to the European Self. While the conception of the Other is rampant in colonial discourse, this discourse is still pervasive, albeit in a modified form. In these headlines, the convergence of her master statuses of ethnicity/race and gender around diseases and mystery may give the audience the impression that racial minority women portend harm and risk to Canadians. Hence, the association of the female body with fear, nationality and anxiety is critical in these headlines and the texts (see appendix). Other key words in the headlines are "risk," "deadly" and "virus" (see appendix).

Quotes and Expressions

Apart from headlines, the choice of words and statements attributed to medical authorities and individuals in the medical institution have a tendency to promote fear. The following are some examples of such expressions, comments and remarks:

> Doctors say they have not been able to specifically determine what is wrong with the seriously ill woman and are assuming the worst. (*Hamilton Spectator* February 6, 2001a)

She is also showing at least some of the symptoms listed under the plan [Health Canada's contingency plan] such as fever, headache, sore throat, shock or bleeding. Doctors say she is not bleeding from her ears or mouth, which are final stage signs of Ebola or other hemorrhagic fevers. However, that doesn't means [sic] she does not have one of the viruses. (*Hamilton Spectator* February 7, 2001a)

When addressing the concerns over the fear of infection by some members of hospital staff, the president of CUPE Local 794 is quoted: "They are scared to death. They're scared not just for themselves, but for their children" (*Hamilton Spectator* February 9, 2001c). Additionally, the *Hamilton Spectator* (February 9, 2001c) comments: "A Hamilton X-ray technician exposed to a Congolese woman with a mystery virus has cancelled her wedding in the Caribbean because she can't leave the country." In a similar vein, the *National Post* writes:

> Five people are considered to be at the highest risk for contracting the unknown infection, including two friends or family members who had contact with her when she arrived, one ambulance attendant and two Henderson staff members who were splashed with the woman's blood, urine, mucus or vomit. They remain on the job. (*National Post* February 9, 2001)

The fact that those "who were splashed with" the bodily fluids of the patient remain on the job is "scary" as it implies a possible spread of an "unknown infection." It also continues to endorse a heightened form of the free floating anxiety as explained by Giddens (1991). In addition, Ungar (1998) argues that the media have a tendency to cause a panic, and also reassure the public by minimizing the intensity of a threat through the "metaphor of otherness." This form of Othering the Ebola virus involves its articulation with the identity of the patient. As some have claimed, in the late modern world, categorical identity serves as the surrogate for safety and community (see Beck 1998; Hier 2003). As is discussed in the next section, the association of the identity of the patient with danger is a way of Othering the risk and, *ipso facto*, assuring the public of its safety.

Imperative of Identity

In his analysis of Western media coverage of Ebola outbreaks in Central Africa, Ungar (1998) claims that the media used Othering as a strategy for reassuring members of Western society that they are safe from external deadly microbes and pathogens. The process of Othering Ebola also entails its linkage to the identity and origin of the patient. This is usually the case in times of uncertainty. As Hier (2003: 15) points out, the quest for certainty in the face of cultural ambiguity has always been at "the expense of the de-legitimization of the Other: the criminalized, racialized, gendered or stigmatized." To this end, the quest for the identity of the patient in the suspected case begins immediately after the presentation of her symptoms. In its first coverage, the *National Post*, for example, is interested in establishing the identity of the patient:

> The woman, who doctors won't identify, arrived at hospital on Sunday in serious condition. They would only say she arrived at Pearson Airport in Toronto on Saturday from the Congo… stayed overnight in the United States before coming to Canada. (*National Post* February 6, 2001)

The other newspapers also show an interest in her identity.

> The woman, whom doctors won't identify, arrived at Henderson Hospital on Sunday in serious condition. They would only say she arrived at Pearson Airport in Toronto on Saturday from the Congo. (*Hamilton Spectator* February 6, 2001b)

The *Globe and Mail* is the first newspaper to disclose the patient's name (see appendix), linking her with a nationality:

> Still, doctors are mystified about what ailment has left [the patient] clinging to life in an intensive-care unit a week after she arrived in Canada from the Democratic Republic of Congo. (*Globe and Mail* February 10, 2001)

It can be acknowledged that the frequency in which a word or phrase appears does not necessarily demonstrate each publication's propensity to delegitimize the non-Ebola patient, but Altheide's (2002: 38–39) point is instructive here:

> When a word is repeated frequently and becomes associated routinely with certain other terms and images, a symbolic linkage is formed… the meanings of two words are suggested by their proximity, their association. Indeed, over time, terms merge in public discourse.

As some of the headlines quoted above show, the nationality of the patient is embedded in the headlines with the word "Ebola." About 5 percent of key words in the *National Post*'s headlines contain "Congolese woman"; 21.4 percent (post-Ebola period) for those of the *Hamilton Spectator*; 6.7 percent (Ebola period) and 22.2 percent (post-Ebola period) for the *Toronto Star*; and 27.3 percent (post-Ebola period) for the *Globe and Mail* (see appendix).

Her name and nationality are often mentioned in close association with the word "Ebola" (see the frequency of her name, nationality and "Ebola" in appendix). Key words such as "Congolese woman," as well as her name, nationality and continent are indicative of how imperative her identity is to the Ebola scare. The reference to her gender and nationality serves to re-affirm the fact that immigrant women are the "outsiders" in relation to Canadians, who are the "insiders" (see Thobani 2000). Her classification as a woman and Congolese "is unthinkable and un-concretizable without its opposite" (Thobani 2000: 283). It is this identification that reminds the readers the threat that minority women pose to the Canadian nation-building project. Hence, the Congolese woman's body was "manipulated to serve [Canadian] national aims" (Murdocca 2003: 29). Expressions such as "the sick woman," "Congolese woman with a mystery illness," "the bug she carries" and "speaking a heavily accented French" serve to distinguish her from the "normal population."

The *Toronto Star*, in its February 9, 2001b, news article, symbolically expresses her dangerousness *vis-à-vis* her physiology thus: "It was cold and dark outside. They had no idea they were carrying a patient who might have a potentially virulent hemorrhagic fever from the heart of Africa." In this comment are implicit relationships between her dark skin colour, the "dark outside," "the heart of Africa" and a threat to humanity from a dark continent. This association is a reminder of Edmund Burke's association of darkness with black skin, which is of relevance to the modern perception and fear of the Other as a threat:

> Perhaps it may appear on enquiry, that blackness and darkness are in some degree painful by their natural operation, independent of any associations whatever. I must observe that the ideas of blackness and darkness are much the same; they differ only in this, that blackness is a more confined idea.
>
> Mr. Cheselden has given us a very curious story of a boy who had been born blind, and continued so until he was thirteen or fourteen years old; he was then couched for a cataract, by which operation he received his sight…Cheselden tells us that the first time the boy saw a black object, it gave him uneasiness; and that some time after, upon accidentally seeing *a Negro woman, he was struck with great horror at the sight.* (cited in Gilroy 1993: 9–10; emphasis added)

The patient's presence as a Black woman with the possibility of carrying a deadly disease was uncomfortable for many. Nonetheless, as Lavani (1995) shows, the construction of Otherness is never fixed, but ambivalent. The patient is also shown some compassion in some coverage. In one instance, the *Toronto Star* (February 10, 2001b) makes the following comments:

What a lonely visit it has been. She lies alone in her own room in the intensive care unit in an unfamiliar country. For roughly five days, every staff member she has come into contact with has approached her wearing a protective face shield, gloves, gown and hair net. Hospital staff say they have delivered few cards, but a friend has been in to see her.

The patient's ambivalent identity as represented in the media is not an anomaly in the representation of Blacks that have assumed popularity/notoriety. Using the concept of a "floating signifier" to describe the representation of African-American basketball players in the media, Wilson (1997) shows how the Black identity can be ambivalent: vacillating between "good black" and "bad black." Black athletes are "good" when they are not doing harm and are expected to be bad when they conform to the dominant stereotypes about them. The patient is also a popular figure, albeit a notorious one to some extent, in her own right. Her identity vacillates between being pitied and being vilified. She personifies threat, danger and evil, but at the same time innocence. On one hand, she is projected as a real folk devil and embodies the negative side of Black as a category. On the other hand, she is a pitiable subject, oblivious and ignorant of the "danger" she is carrying.

Immigration and Health Risks

Unlike the other newspapers, the *Toronto Star* brings up the issue around immigration and health early in its coverage of the case. In the other newspapers, the issue of immigration and health does not get coverage until later. One of the early *Toronto Star* news articles, published on February 6, 2001, begins by stating that the patient arrived from Africa. The second paragraph adds: "The woman, whose identity and nationality is not known arrived at Toronto's Pearson International Airport on Saturday from the Congo via New York, where she stayed Friday night" (*Toronto Star* February 6, 2001a). The article concludes by bringing up the topic of her immigration status in a way that connotes disfavour: "Immigration officials noted that Canada does not do medical screening for legitimate visitors to the country, unless they appear ill on arrival." The news article closes by quoting an immigration official as saying: "There is no way you can insulate Canada from the rest of the world" (*Toronto Star* February 6, 2001a). In another news report, the *Toronto Star* reports that the "news that the female patient is a visitor to Canada prompted calls by Ontario Health Minister Elizabeth Witmer to review the federal immigration screening program, which appears to be allowing people with serious illness into the country" (*Toronto Star* February 7, 2001b). One of the *Toronto Star*'s headlines reads:

Can't "shrink wrap" borders, Caplan says, Witmer stresses importance of "safety of the public" (*Toronto Star* February 7, 2001)

This news article "moderates" a debate between the Ontario Minister
of Health and the Citizenship and Immigration Minister, Elinor Caplan.
Minister Caplan is quoted as saying: "Medical screening of all visitors to
Canada wouldn't be realistic." The news report adds: "'It is impossible to
shrink wrap our borders,' Caplan told reporters who asked about her department's handling of visitors who might be sick." Furthermore, the federal
minister is quoted as saying: "We live in a global world, Canadians are on
the move and traveling internationally. Hundreds of thousands of people
visit Canada each year for short periods of time" (*Toronto Star* February 7,
2001a). While the minister's reaction is not unfavourable to immigration,
the audience is being exposed to the negative aspect of immigration, most
especially how immigration can serve as conveyor of diseases to Canada.
Critical perspectives of the issues as they relate to underlying social inequality
and injustice meted out to the patient and those close to her, or what Knight
(2004: 139) refers to as "alternative and ordinary voices," are missing in this
coverage.

The *Toronto Star* news article also presents the position of the Ontario
Minister of Health as follows: "At Queen's Park, Ontario Minster Elizabeth
Witmer said there needs to be an immediate review of the federal immigration
screening program." She is quoted: "We need to carefully review the current
procedures that are in place and take a look at what additional measures
may be required to ensure the safety of the public…. It is important that we
protect the public." Also, the idea of "screening" by this public official appears
to connect immigration with health risks. Given that most new immigrants
are from non-European countries and are distinguished somatically from the
dominant population, the concept of "screening" can make members of the
public, who have already equated "immigrants" with "non-Whites" (see Li
2003), feel that immigration from certain parts of the world is a health risk
to Canadians. There appears to be a widespread belief that Canada is not
only letting too many immigrants in but also letting them in without proper
medical screening. One of the journalists interviewed for the study was very
frank about what he perceived as indiscriminate admittance of too many
immigrants to Canada without proper medical screening. In his words:

> I think one of the things I would have been happy with is if we could have
> established the federal government's role sooner, and the difficulties with
> the screening process for it really concerned me a lot. It seems to be that
> there were issues around the processing of prospective immigrants that
> didn't make sense to me; they were processing far too many people,
> far too quickly, and that seems to me to be one of the issues that I'm not

sure was explored enough. In terms of the importance of this story, to me, [it] wasn't the individual, it was that there were bigger problems with the system, if I can put it that way. There were larger systemic problems that might have implications for more people in the future, maybe next time we won't be so lucky.

For this journalist, the problem was not only about not "screening" prospective immigrants but also about Canada being "overpopulated" by immigrants. Regarding the concern over immigrants "overpopulating" Canada, Thobani (2000) finds links between immigration and concern over population growth in her analysis of discussion texts concerning immigration and social security prepared for public consultations by the Canadian government in 1994.

News reports on medical coverage and immigration come later in the other newspapers. The suspected case is also used to criticize the health care system and inadequate funding for Canadian hospitals. The *Globe and Mail* uses the case to recall that Canadian residents also do not pay their bills. Its headline of March 14, 2001, reads: "Ontarians leave trail of hospital debts too, Suspected Ebola victim's tab unpaid, but official says residents also fail to pay up." The article makes the following comments:

> But the unpaid bills for the uninsured visitor to Canada — who was given experimental drugs and treated for 27 days in an intensive-care unit — have become news despite the fact that many hospitals deal with bad debts from Canadian residents every day. (*Globe and Mail* March 14, 2001)

The spokesperson for the Hamilton Sciences Corporation is quoted as saying: "At the end of the day, we have more bad debts from Ontario residents than from visitors... visitors are part of the problem, but not the whole problem" (*Globe and Mail* March 14, 2001). This case has provided a space for expressing the public's dissatisfaction with the reigning political economy of neo-liberalism. This indicates that the media are not simply a "mouthpiece" for the powerful.

The case also leads to a call for immigration reforms. This concern is expressed in a *National Post* article which draws attention to another official news source — the president of the Ontario Medical Association, Dr. Albert Schumacher: "the expensive case has the president of the Ontario Medical Association calling on the federal government to take responsibility for visitors it allows into the country and to cover the costs" (*National Post* March 13, 2001). Schumacher, is further quoted as saying: "We don't have any policy in this country to make sure visitors from abroad carry medical insurance of any sort." He continues, "When our government decides to receive people here in the country, they need to make sure they've made provisions for care" (*National Post* March 13, 2001). The news article further comments:

> The federal and provincial governments never pay for the health care of foreign visitors, who are expected to pay for themselves. However, nothing is done before they enter the country to ensure they have health coverage or the money to pay for medical emergencies. The issue is significant because hospitals do not have extra cash to cover the outstanding bills. They have to pay for it out of their tight annual budgets. (*National Post* March 13, 2001)

Jay Robb, the spokesperson for the Hamilton Health Sciences Corporation is quoted as saying: "Our budgets are so razor-thin that we're committed to finding $15-million in [cost] savings. There isn't a whole lot of money to go around." The newspaper makes additional comments: "It is unknown exactly how much this case will cost the corporation but the bill is currently $60,000 and growing" (*National Post* March 13, 2001). The frustration over inadequate health care funding is deflected to the immigration/visitor status of the patient. The patient thus becomes a symbolic expression of public concern and anxiety over declining social welfare.

The media focus on the debate between the two public functionaries, Elizabeth Witmer and Elinor Caplan, relates to what Rose refers to as the "politicization of danger," which often involves the "management or exclusion of dangerous populations" (Rose 2002: 199), rather than a focus on what Fraser (2005) refers to as an injustice of "cultural misrecognition" of members of ethno-religious communities. In this particular case, medical diagnosis is suppressed in the discourse even though doctors ruled out Ebola as a reason for the patient's illness.

Crime and Immigration

Pratt and Valverde (2002) note that the Canadian public is often suspicious of refugees and has perceived them as "masters of confusion" and as potential criminals. The development of a theme of crime and suspicion in the latter coverage of the non-Ebola event seems to have affirmed the pre-existing negative perception of the Other. On March 3, 2001, the *National Post* carried the following headline on its front page: "'Ebola' victim investigated for diamond smuggling: sick woman caused panic." In the days that followed, other newspapers joined in developing the story.

Although the theme of crime appears in the latter part of the coverage, a close reading of the overall coverage of the event reveals that suspicion develops in tandem with other themes in a non-obvious way. Before discussing the specific crime-related coverage, it is important to point out journalists' perception of the patient as a suspect of some crime. The *Hamilton Spectator* (February 10, 2001d) makes the following comments:

> Federal officials have said [the patient] arrived on a business visa and reporters have been told she was due to travel to Montreal for a conference involving the energy sector. *Efforts to find such a conference through Tourism Montreal or Hydro Quebec were unsuccessful.* (emphasis added)

Interviews with journalists further reveal some suspicion:

> There are so many irregularities around, or there appeared to be, I should say, some irregularities around why she came here, and what she told Canadian officials she was here for. That it looked as though she was coming for as I recall a conference or something in Montreal but her arriving in Hamilton, the timing of it made it look as though she wasn't going to the conference in Montreal at all, and that made everyone suspicious so it appears as though she was trying to hide her real purpose for coming here. That raises the question why diamond smuggling was one kind of an answer.

The journalist who makes the above remarks is a crime investigator. He describes his process as follows:

> When journalists talk about investigative reporting they usually mean stories that are more complex, where the truths are perhaps hidden or shielded and you have to spend more time to get at that information so you might work for weeks or months to produce a single story. I would go out with a specific goal, such as where did she live? Find out where she lived, talk to her neighbours to see when she got here, what you can find out about how she got here, and what she did when she was here.

That the first news linking her to diamond smuggling was run by the *National Post* is not surprising, given the undercurrent of suspicion. Henry and Tator (2002: 120–37) have shown in their analysis that the *National Post* categorized Tamils in Toronto as "terrorists" and "criminals" and that the *National Post* is blatantly anti-immigration. One of the ways that the *National Post* problematizes immigration, according to Henry and Tator (2002), is by racializing crime. The headline of the first breaking news on crime in the newspaper reads:

> "Ebola" victim investigated for diamond smuggling: sick woman caused panic (*National Post* March 3, 2001)

While it is the *National Post* that first ran the news, other newspapers' accounts are similar. All the newspapers eventually published stories implying that the motive for her coming to Canada was diamond smuggling. Her nationality in association with Ebola and smuggling made headlines. The following are more examples:

"Ebola" patient in smuggling probe:Left hospital Friday, went into hiding (*Hamilton Spectator* March 5, 2001)

Congolese woman draws RCMP's interest; Mounties will meet Immigration officials to discuss Hamilton visit (*Hamilton Spectator* March 6, 2001)

RCMP rule out probe of victim in Ebola scare (*Globe and Mail* March 7, 2001)

The representation of the woman as a suspect of crime is congruent with van Dijk's (1993b) assertion that topics such as crime are ethnicized. That is, crime becomes a major topic that is cross-articulated with race/ethnicity in the media (van Dijk 1993b: 249). Expressions that characterize her as an ardent criminal, such as: "the Congolese woman at the source of an Ebola scare last month has been released from hospital, and has gone into hiding amid news reports she is being investigated for links to a diamond smuggling" (*Toronto Star* March 5, 2001) and "an official said her condition could not have been caused by swallowing diamonds, a tactic sometimes used by smugglers" (*National Post* March 3, 2001) are found in the newspaper articles examined.

In the *Hamilton Spectator* of February 9, 2001, a 2.5 by 3.8 inch photograph of the house where the patient stayed was featured on the front cover with the following caption: "A Congolese woman with a mysterious illness apparently stayed in an apartment in this building for a short time on the weekend." In the centrespread of the newspaper, the house is also featured with a police officer standing in the front, with the caption: "A police officer talks with a man yesterday outside a Steven Street residence where a Congolese woman with a mysterious illness is believed to have stayed." The article that accompanies a photograph states: "When [the patient] arrived in front of the run down building in a seedy downtown neighbourhood, she was exhausted and confused" (*Hamilton Spectator* February 9, 2001b). To further stress her low socio-economic status, the article notes: "[she] was seeking her hostess, a friend from the Congo who had been renting the small, $350-a month apartment for a year" (*Hamilton Spectator* February 9, 2001b). In semiotics, photographs are texts (see Barthes 1972; Bryman 2004: 393–94). They signify important meanings beyond and beneath the manifest meanings of texts. Photographs, for example, can be read as a sign and linked to broader cultural and ideological themes. The publication of where she stayed in the form of a photograph, with police presence, may incur in news readers an image of a crime scene. Her representation in this instance assumes a number of negative stereotypes that Wilson (1997) refers to as "bad Blacks" (as opposed to "good Blacks"): poor, crime-prone, filthy and threatening.

Substitution and Anti-Racial-Diversity Subtexts

There is no single reference to "race" or "Black" in the media coverage. The terms of reference are "Congo" and "Africa" and are in connection to the etiology of Ebola and other deadly diseases (see appendix). It is not unusual for the media to couch views that are anti-racial diversity in non-racial terms. Li (2001) has addressed this in his analysis of anti-immigration rhetoric in public consultations organized by Canadian Immigration and Citizenship. In his analysis of opinion polls, government documents and the media, he argues that intolerance for the immigration of people of non-European descent is expressed in race-neutral ways:

> To study racial discourses involves accepting racism as an everyday phenomenon that is manifested in a benign version, often without the label of racism. This version is communicated in coded language so that on appearance it is not race or racism at stake, but in essence it carries a message about unbridgeable differences of people premised upon values, traditions, and always of life subsumed under skin colour or other superficial features. (Li 2001: 81)

Further, words like "diversity" and "visible minorities" serve as a sobriquet for racially different groups. Li states:

> Racism can be articulated in an elusive and covert manner in a democratic society precisely because the construction of race is not scientifically grounded, and the absence of a scientific standard provides flexibility in racial signification. (Li 2001: 79)

However, van Dijk (1993b) has noted that texts with racist undertones can be detected by a technique he refers to as "implications," which are

> meanings (propositions) that are not explicitly expressed in the text but may be inferred from words or sentences in the text, as well as from the mental models constructed during understanding. Indeed, it is sometimes more important to specify what is *not* said by the text than what is actually expressed. In many respects, media texts are ideological icebergs, of which only the tip is visible to the reader (van Dijk 1993b: 256, emphasis original).

In this case, direct allusions are not made to Blacks or racial minorities as a problem. However, the racist connotations of the coverage can be detected by the implications of some expressions and ideas. For example, the *Hamilton Spectator* (February 6, 2001a), comments:

> It was a turn-around for a department that kept quiet when a man from the Dominican Republic with multidrug resistant tuberculosis exposed more than 1,200 people in Hamilton to the deadly disease.

Here an active voice is used to establish a relationship between a problem (health risk) and its agent (the man from the Dominican Republic overtly portrayed as the agent of risk and blame). This use of active voice makes much stronger the association between the man from the Dominican Republic and all the connotations of immigrants of racial minority groups being a risk. Further, by implication, the subtext from the above newspaper text is that non-Whites pose risks to the lives of Canadians. To be specific, it is more probable that a citizen of the Dominican Republic would be of African or Asian descent. It is contended that such a connotation leaves little room to think of "a man from the Dominican Republic" as White. As empirical studies by Washer (2004) and Shah (2001) have shown, the mechanism for Othering involves associating deadly contagious diseases with racial minorities.

Like Li (2001), Miles (1988) shows in his study of Britain's post-war immigration policy that racism can be coded by politicians and the public in non-racist terms. Miles (1988: 13) claims:

> As an element of commonsense, the idea of "race" need not necessarily be explicitly articulated for it to have real effects on the political process. By definition, commonsense is all those "taken for granted" ideas and "facts" which shape the manner in which problems are defined and solutions are sought. This can be done without the idea of "race" ever being articulated. And even when the idea of "race" is explicitly articulated, its commonsense status ensures that such usage does not require legitimation or explanation.

The following newspaper quote is an archetypical example of race-neutral expressions of racism in the coverage of the non-Ebola panic:

> A source said one of the community members who might be at risk attends a downtown Hamilton school. A staff member at Ecole Notre Dame, a French elementary school, said they have two students who recently arrived from Congo — but neither had been contacted by public-health officials. In Hamilton there are as many as 300 residents originally from the Democratic Republic of Congo,

according to a representative for the Settlement and Integration Services Organization (*Globe and Mail* February 8, 2001a).

Although there is no direct reference to "race" or "Black" in the above quote, it has some racial connotations. The reference to "two students" who just arrived from the Congo and are in the community implies that the public should look out for every dark-skinned kid, as the audience would imagine the Congolese to be Black rather than White or Asian. However, since it is very difficult to identify the Congolese from other Blacks, for the purpose of isolation, it then implies, by default, that every Black person in Hamilton is a potential carrier of the deadly virus.

van Dijk (2000: 40) notes that "much of the information in discourse, and hence also in news reports, is implicit, and supplied by the recipients on the basis of their knowledge of the context of the world." Derogatory or denigrating statements about racial minorities in the media are not explicitly stated "because of social norms, and for reasons of impression management. For instance, many negative things about minorities may not be stated explicitly, and thus are conveyed 'between the lines'" (van Dijk 2000: 40). Although the newspapers examined do not categorically claim that the Congolese are carriers of the deadly disease, the association between race and contagious diseases is implicit in some of the media texts. In regards to whether the patient's illness is caused by malaria or a more serious virus, the *Hamilton Spectator* writes that "she was diagnosed with malaria, but tropical disease specialists concluded she had to be suffering from something else as well." The newspaper goes on to quote a doctor as saying:

> It's unlikely that everything she has would be caused by that degree of malaria. Apparently in that part of the world (Africa), it's not unusual for people to be entirely healthy walking around like you or I with that level of a parasite load. (*Hamilton Spectator* February 9, 2001b)

This quote seems to imply that the risk the patient poses is greater because visible signs of the problem may remain latent for longer periods of time among some populations rather than others. The text Otherizes the disease because it implies that Canadians are at a greater health risk than people from "that part of the world." Moreover, the comparison further implies that those who look like Africans are natural hosts of deadly viruses, as compared to "you or I," the Canadians, as stated. Despite whatever scientific validity that this statement may have, it may unwittingly reinforce in the public the perception of racial differences and attribute contagious diseases to phenotypical variations. This statement reminds one of Hall's (1997) notion of naturalization, which is "a representational strategy designed to *fix* 'difference,' and thus *secure it forever*" (Hall 1997: 245, emphasis original).

Agenda Setting: Editorials and Letters to the Editor

Two letters to the editor regarding the non-Ebola case were published by the *Hamilton Spectator*, one by the *Toronto Star*, one by the *National Post* and none by the *Globe and Mail*. The relatively few letters to the editor, given the high level of attention paid to the case, affirm the weakness of alternative discourse and acceptance of the dominant discourse by the readership (Knight 2001: 83; see also Galtung and Ruge 1981).

On February 9, 2001, the *Hamilton Spectator* published two letters to the editor: one from Niagara Falls, Ontario, and the other from Calgary, Alberta. They take somewhat different standpoints. The first letter sets to oppose Immigration Minister Elinor Caplan's comments on the case, opening with: "With respect to concerns over the latest disease carrier entering Canada, Immigration Minister Elinor Caplan has said: 'it's impossible to set up a policy of testing everyone. We have over 200 million people crossing our borders annually. It is impossible to shrink-wrap our borders.'" It continues: "Agreed. But the immigration minister can take effective action far short of that." The writer then identifies two groups with "the highest probability of being carriers of new and deadly diseases to Canada." They are: "refugee claimants released into the general population as soon as their initial paperwork is done" and "those arriving from high-risk locations." The letter concludes that "both groups are identifiable" and states that it is imperative to protect Canada from the danger posed by these groups (*Hamilton Spectator*, February 9, 2001g).

"Refugee claimants," singled out by this writer, can be read as substitution for racial minority immigrants. Just as Li (2003: 46) asserts that in the folk version of an immigration problem "there is a considerable overlap between the concepts 'immigrants' and 'non-Whites' or 'visible minorities,'" this writer may be using "refugee claimant" as a code phrase for racial minorities. "High-risk locations" refer to the non-Western countries of Asia and Africa, where it is presumed that deadly diseases are preponderant. The subtexts of the letter writer's proposition are that the immigration of non-Whites to Canada is a threat to Canadians and that racial profiling is an effective measure for guaranteeing Canadians' safety.

The second letter acknowledges the reality of crossing borders in the global age and the possible presence of contagious diseases in Canada. In a letter titled "Let's start from overseas" (*Hamilton Spectator*, February 9, 2001h), the writer states: "For our protection in Canada, we must treat victims overseas as well as here." The writer believes infectious diseases, such as Ebola, TB, malaria and HIV/AIDS are related to poverty and underdevelopment.

The letter supports increased government spending on foreign aid for the eradication of poverty through "basic education, primary health care and nutrition."

The letter to the editor published by the *Toronto Star* on February 9, 2001, points out "the difficulty of shrink wrapping the Canadian border," as expressed by Witmer. In the view of the writer, "shrink wrapping" the border is not commercially viable. However, the writer states, "I do, however, believe that it would be possible to target high-risk areas, which to me, seem to include The Democratic Republic of Congo." The letter then identifies those who need not be screened by the Canadian government: "You cannot expect to screen everyone who comes across the border from the U.S., or flies in from Europe and other such locations." The writer then adds, "It is not economically feasible and would definitely not help tourism." The letter is concluded with the following comments:

> Canada is as multicultural as countries come, and with borders becoming more open, such as those within the European Union, the fact remains that diseases are an ever-present threat, where the only means of protection is to target the high-risk areas.

This discourse is consistent with Miles' (1988) notion of "race/immigration dualism." In this case, the threat of a disease is equated to the immigration of people from certain parts of the world. The subtext is that immigrants and visitors from "high-risk areas," like the Democratic Republic of Congo, are a danger to the health of Canadians and are *ipso facto* an "immigration problem." The delegitimization of people from "high-risk areas," like the Democratic Republic of Congo, through border control implies racialization. As Miles (1989) explains, racialization involves situations where social relationships between people have been organized based on the signification of human physical characteristics "in such way as to define and construct differentiated social collectivities" (Miles 1989: 75). Although the letter from the *Toronto Star* does not allude to "race," racialization can occur in the absence of the term (see Satzewich 1998b: 32). Comparing people coming across the border from Europe and the U.S. with those from "high-risk areas" like the Democratic Republic of Congo entails the process of signification of physical difference, which is equivalent to racialization.

Letters to the editor are normally a reaction to op-ed pieces, including the editorial, and hard news that have been previously published by the newspaper. On February 8, 2001, the day prior to the publication of the above letters to the editor, the *Hamilton Spectator* ran an editorial. Although the editorial lacks the journalistic ideals of "objectivity" and "balance," it exerts considerable influence over how readers make meaning of the events around them. van Dijk (1993b: 266) claims that editors in Western countries use the editorials to speak to the White audience. If so, this editorial may be aiming to set an anti-immigration agenda in the way it constructs a discourse of health insecurity around immigration. It opens with the following:

> Fear and anxiety for ourselves, our children and neighbors. Growing unease about our government's ability to keep us safe from new and frightening diseases. Immeasurable stress on our already stretched health system. Intolerance and mistrust of people from other parts of the world... and at the centre, a critically ill woman who came to Canada on business, perhaps carrying a deadly passenger.

The editorial continues: "Surely, this isn't what Marshall McLuhan had in mind when he talked about the global village." It further states: "News that a seriously ill Congolese woman being treated at Henderson General Hospital is probably not suffering from the Ebola virus is welcome, but doesn't lessen the gravity of this situation." It adds: "the clinical specifics of this case are less important than the lessons we can take from it."

The editorial spells out two lessons that need to be learned. One is that while globalization has made the world smaller and more interdependent, diseases like Ebola are still a threat because they are closer to "home" (i.e., Canada). The editorial compares the possible devastation of diseases like Ebola to the ones wrought on the Aboriginals of North America by the Europeans centuries earlier: "like North American Aboriginal people exposed to smallpox and influenza by European visitors hundreds of years ago, we are players on the global health stage, whether we like it or not." The subtext of this message is that just as the "European visitors'" incursion to North America was deadly to the population, contemporary "immigration" (and "visitors") signals a related danger to the Canadian population. The second lesson that can be gleaned from this case, according to this writer, is that the "crisis" must be used as a learning experience "to improve public policy and raise awareness." It also suggests that "stereotypes, fear, or intolerance" should not prevent people from discussing the issue. The editorial concludes with a note of warning: "There will be a next time. This may be a North American first, but it won't be the last time a community struggles with a situation like this. Let's set a good example." This conclusion sounds apocalyptic in the way it predicts a future tragedy. Moreover, the term "community," as it is used by the editorial, is ambiguous (see Goldring 1996 for discussion). Its usage in this editorial allows readers to interpret the term in different ways. For example, some readers might opt to construe the term "community" as equivalent to exclusion and insulation. The allusion to the devastating effects of influenza and smallpox on the North American Aboriginal population is very similar to Washer's (2004) findings in his study of the British press coverage of SARS. Washer (2004) finds that the media invoked earlier epidemics with catastrophic outcomes, as opposed to the ones with fewer deaths, to emphasize the serious threat of SARS to the British population.

"Opinion discourses," including editorials, op-ed articles and guest columns, Greenberg (2000) claims, are important in the construction of the Other. Unlike hard news texts, opinion discourses have a potential to recruit news readers because they "possess a unique idiomatic character that 'speaks' directly to the readership in a way that is familiar, habitual, and reliable" (Greenberg 2000: 529). The use of pronouns such as "we" and "our" in the *Hamilton Spectator*'s editorial is a direct appeal to members of society. These pronouns are meant to tap into the "collective conscience" of external threat. Thus, the *Hamilton Spectator*'s editorial piece appeals to average members of society — parents, neighbours and citizens. De Cillia et al. (1999: 160) refer to this mode of recruiting the audience as "constructive strategies," which "are all persuasive linguistic devices which help invite identification and solidarity with the 'we-group,' which, however, simultaneously implies distancing from and marginalization of 'others.'"

Risks pertain to anxiety about the future. According to Beck (1992:33), "risks have something to do with anticipation, with destruction that has not yet happened but is threatening, and of course in that sense risks are already real today." The statement "there will be a next time" echoes Beck's notion of risks regarding the possibility of future danger, judging from the present. Unlike the editorial of the *Hamilton Spectator*, the editorial of the *National Post* of February 9, 2001, aims to allay public fear, but like the former it also sounds its own note of warning about future risks. Its opening statement is: "Breathe easy. Lab results released this week indicate that a Congolese woman receiving treatment in a Hamilton, Ont., hospital does not, as first feared, suffer from the dreaded Ebola virus." Following these sentences, like the editorial of the *Hamilton Spectator*, it warns of impending health risks through international migration: "But it is probably only a matter of time before a visitor to Canada does. And when that happens, it is important we avoid hysteria." Two points are worthy of note here. First, the statement "it is probably only a matter of time before a visitor to Canada does" bring a "deadly disease" excludes the possibility that the potential carrier could be a Canadian. Second, the allusion to a possible future presence of a virus like Ebola in Canada, similar to that of the *Hamilton Spectator* editorial, is a call for state intervention in the form of immigration control and the screening of certain immigrants.

Knight (2004: 139) notes that alternative points may compete with dominant values in the media, but towards an attainment of hegemony. Knight's point is apt and is relevant to the analysis of the two letters to the editor carried by the *Hamilton Spectator*. As discussed above, the two letters do differ in perspective. Contrary to the position of the first letter, the second letter introduces discourses of "development" and "hygienization" to dilute the dominant discourse of immigration and health hazards. It proposes increased foreign aid and the eradication of poverty as a solution to global health risks and insecurity (see Garrett 2000). Nevertheless, the letter is consistent with the dominant terms of reference, that is, a perception of deadly disease from the "outside," the Other. This letter, coupled with the "anti-racial-diversity" letter, may give the impression of journalistic neutrality or impartiality to the *Hamilton Spectator* — the publication of two letters with opposing views. However, the letters do not divest the newspaper of its ideological project because the two letters converge on the point that Canada is a possible target of foreign deadly diseases. Overall, the differing positions may exonerate the newspaper of partiality. This is in essence ideological or hegemonic as Knight (2004) points out. A similar analysis of ideological work and discursive practices is provided by Greenberg and Wilson (2006) in their examination of newspaper coverage of risk, youth and moral panic.

The convergence of themes in the four mainstream newspapers examined for this study is congruent with Galtung and Ruge's (1981) point that negative news will be more consensual and unambiguous in the sense that people can easily agree on an interpretation of events constructed as negative.[4] Based on the significant influence of the mass media on the formation of racial identities in modern societies, some have argued that racism comes from the top and trickles down to the bottom (Cox 1948). One may be tempted to believe that media representation of events has a direct relationship on how people behave. From this line of reasoning, it can be inferred that the representation of the non-Ebola event has a direct effect on the Canadian public. Though the media may have a powerful influence on public opinion, they do not impose their views on the readership. Rather, people relate to media content based on their fragmented subject positions or identities (Hay 1996; Kitzinger 1998a,b).

Using the Gramscian notion of "traces," Hall (1981) illustrates how old stereotypes about Africa and Blacks have been modified to suit contemporary circumstances. The mass media continue to employ these old stereotypes, albeit in their modified form, to reinforce existing inequalities between the Self and the Other. These "traces" have their source in slavery, colonial discourse and observable material imbalances between Europeans and Africans. Pieterse (1992) uses the fundraising campaigns by agencies for relief aid for Africa to illustrate how a particular stereotype about Africa becomes reproduced and gains acceptance in the West. The media's constant reference to a "Congolese woman" with "Ebola" can reinforce in the public an image that may already exist; thus further reinforcing existing stereotypes. While content analysis cannot make a linkage between these "traces" and a contemporary event like the Ebola coverage, the structure of the coverage privileges a particular way of viewing the issues of immigration, race and diseases and, as such, provides the audience with information that is already ideologically inflected.

Notes

1. This chapter is a greatly expanded version of the article by myself and Nicole Neverson, "There Will Be A Next Time": Media Discourse about an "Apocalyptic" Vision of Immigration, Racial Diversity, and Health Risks," published in *Canadian Ethnic Studies* 39 (1 & 2), 2007: 79–105.

2. The interviews with journalists that appear in this chapter occurred between March 2003 and May 2003. The journalists quoted here were interviewed in their offices in Hamilton, Ontario.

3. "You" here means "anyone." That is, contemporary risks are represented in the media as ever-present and ubiquitous.

4. At first glance, it appears that the four newspapers examined in this study have varied ideological orientations and differentiated audiences and market niches. For example, the *National Post* is popularly considered to be more critical of immigration and racial diversity than other newspapers (see Henry and Tator 2002). But beneath the surface there do not appear to be appreciable differences in coverage between the four newspapers. While some themes appear more or less frequently in the newspapers, they all single out the Other — an immigrant — as the problem. Their seemingly different accounts of events, nevertheless, converge to reproduce the dominant stereotypes of the Other. In regard to this convergence, Hall et al.'s (1978: 61) view that the media do not necessarily represent "the vast pluralistic range of voices" but "a range within certain distinct ideological limits" is relevant to this case.

Chapter 4

"The Unrespectable View of Society"

Competing Claims

Media researchers often rely on voice quotes attributed to representatives of various strata of society to show the unequal distribution of power and status in that society (Knight 2001; Greenberg and Knight 2004). On the basis of source quotes, media analysts can demonstrate how access to the media translates into access to power, which van Dijk (1993a: 256) phrases as "parallelism between social power and discourse access." However, recent studies have shown that the power elites do not always have the monopoly over the control of media space as the powerless can redefine situations in mainstream and alternative media outlets (see McRobbie 1994; Hier 2002a; Greenberg and Knight 2004). Non-elites can redefine situations in the media not only because access to the media has become liberalized (McRobbie 1994), but also because claims makers can attract media attention if they are well organized, creative, strategic and dramatic (see Carroll and Ratner 1999). Organizations and social groups that can package their stories with emotional appeals now enjoy media coverage in an age of "increased feelings of risk and panic about modern life" (Wardle 2006: 530). Although the alternative media (Skinner 2006) — the media that provide a range of perspectives that are not covered in the profit-driven mainstream media — and the new media (Scatamburlo-D'Annibale and Boin 2006) — Internet-related forms of media that include cell phones, blogs and chat rooms — are outlets for ordinary citizens to contest their misrepresentation and underrepresentation in the mainstream media, these avenues might not be as effective as have been claimed by the recent literature (see Hier 2002; Wilson and Atkinson 2005) in the redefinition of situations. Social factors of class, ethnicity and culture still constrain some citizens from redefining their representation in the media.

Knight (1998a) identifies three types of news sources: official, ordinary and alternate sources. Based on Knight's (1998a: 121-123) typologies, doctors, immigration officials and union members constitute the official sources of the Ebola scare as their information is treated by the media as credible, rational and objective. Official sources, according to Knight (1998a: 121), are "the primary sources and thus representatives of dominant institutions." For this reason, Hall et al. (1978) claim that the mass media reproduce power inequalities in such a way that unequal power relations become routinized and taken for granted. Ordinary news sources counteract the official sources. They "personify the effects of bad news, the actual or potential victims who are exposed to harm, suffering, or deprivation" (Knight 1998a: 121). These are the voices of members of the Black community. Alternative news sources are those of social movements and activist groups who are concerned with issues of equity and justice. Their discontents are usually "directed against the institutions that official sources represent, and on behalf of ordinary victims" (Knight 1998a: 121). Unlike ordinary sources, Knight posits that alternative news sources are more or less organized and often have the power of collective resources, including their own "experts," and thus sustain a more recurrent presence in the news. Members of the Black community had their own "experts," who were non-practising medical doctors, professionals and paraprofessionals, but they were not formally organized to constitute an alternative source to the official source. Apart from a hierarchy of news sources, Loseke (2003) states that there is also a hierarchy of access, in which institutions and individuals with status and power have greater access to the media than those with less power and status.

This chapter shows the futility of the Congolese and other members of the Black community in charting an alternative and popular course for the non-Ebola narrative based on the aforementioned social indicators of culture, ethnicity and class. Some members of the Canadian public might have found the translation of Ebola into an immigration problem convincing because in the framing of the event alternative and ordinary voices are obscured. The media screened out the voices of the Black community in order to make the problematization of immigration and racial diversity in Canadian society effective, convincing and adequate. There is a hierarchy of credibility among claims makers. At the top are scientists (Loseke 2003: 36) and those connected with official institutions (Knight 1998a). Some claims fail to persuade the audience not because they lack truth value, but because they are articulated by groups and organizations that are low on the scale of credibility. For example, in the non-Ebola panic, the medical claims occupy a higher level of credibility than the competing claims of lay persons and non-practising physicians in the Black community. While the previous chapter is a comprehensive review and analysis of the dominant frame — the construction of the non-Ebola panic as a problem of immigration and racial diversity — this chapter provides the construction of the non-Ebola event by members of the Black community. Their narratives represent what Knight (1998a) refers to as "ordinary voices" that were suppressed in the media. In addition to the ordinary voices of members of the Black community, the relationship between the institutions of medicine and media are given space in this chapter.[1] The racialization of the non-Ebola panic succeeds partly because Blacks were underrepresented in key institutions of society and partly because they lacked the *savoir-faire* (Poulantzas 1978) necessary to translate emotions into what Fiske (1996) refers to as "media events." As Fiske (1996: 2) explains, "events do happen, but ones that are not mediated do not count, or, at least, count only in their immediate locales."

The Medical Framework

Members of the medical community did not agree on the diagnosis of Ebola. Dissenting perspectives also came from laypersons and non-practising medical doctors of African descent. The substance of the scientific community's version of the incident comes from three sources: a publication in a science journal by specialists, two of them being infectious diseases specialists directly involved in the case (see Loeb et al. 2003); documents produced by the director of media communications for Henderson Incorporation (Vallentin 2002); and interviews with two of the doctors who attended to the patient. The case was presented to the emergency department of a university hospital (McMaster University) on February 4, 2001, the day after the patient arrived in Canada from the Democratic Republic of Congo via Europe and the U.S. According to Loeb et al. (2003), on presentation the patient had a temperature of 38.5 degrees Celsius. It was observed that "there was bleeding from her nose, mouth, and urinary tract," but "there were no conjunctival, meningeal, or focal neurologic abnormalities" (Loeb et al. 2003: 281).

On February 5, 2001, the day following her presentation at the emergency unit, her condition was assessed by

> a specialist in tropical medicine whose differential diagnosis included meningococcemia, bacterial sepsis, dengue fever, leptospirosis, rickettsial disease, viral encephalitis, and VHF. Congo-Crimean hemorrhagic fever, yellow fever, Lassa fever, Ebola hemorrhagic fever, and Marburg virus hemorrhagic fever were all considered possibilities. (Loeb et al. 2003)

According to the medical report, malaria was part of the broader diagnosis, and the patient was treated for it. However, given her "low level of parasitemia," malaria was considered as an inadequate cause of her illness. Since hemorrhagic fever was suspected, Health Canada's contingency plan for viral hemorrhagic fever (VHF) was implemented for the first time.

Three categories of at-risk individuals are identified by the hospital, based on the Canadian contingency plan for hemorrhagic fevers. They are high-risk contacts, close contacts and casual contacts. The first category comprised three physicians: one was exposed to the patient's saliva, and the other two to her blood. Twenty-two close contacts include sixteen individuals who were health care workers and six laboratory workers. The third category consists of sixty health care workers and individuals who are at the intensive care units, with no direct contact with the patient, before the patient was isolated (see Loeb et al. 2003: 281–82).

Over the course of her hospitalization, different tests were done to determine the specific hemorrhagic fever responsible for her illness. On the third day, results confirmed Ebola and Marburg viruses to be negative. Over time, her condition deteriorated and a plan was put in place for her impending death. In the words of Loeb et al. (2003: 283):

> Arrangements for consent were made should an autopsy be needed. However, local pathologists said they would refuse to perform the autopsy based on their perceptions that the facilities were not suitably equipped for such a case. Arrangements therefore were made with another tertiary-care facility should the need for an autopsy arise.

On the fifth day of her hospitalization, tests for other possible VHFs were negative, and, over a period of two weeks, she gradually recovered and was discharged. From the medical perspective, "no etiologic agent was detected despite extensive testing" (Loeb et al. 2003: 283).

The high level of attention the case generated is described by Jeff Vallentin, the director of media communications for Henderson Hospital, in a document titled, *Managing a Mystery Virus*. In the document he explains:

> Two news conferences were held on day two (Tuesday), and one on each of the next three days as the situation evolved. It was Tuesday morning when reporters from most major news outlets, including a fleet of satellite trucks, converged on the Henderson expecting to set up camp. To accommodate the technology and the number of reporters, I designated the hospital's cafeteria as the centre for media conferences, the place for the latest information, and a holding area for media. To protect the privacy of our patients and to minimize disruption in the hospital, I requested additional security staff to assist in restricting media access to the rest of the hospital and, in particular, the Intensive Care Unit where our patient lay fighting for her life. (Vallentin 2002: 6)

The media attention to the case is no surprise; even in the face of medical experts' claims of "infinitesimal" risks, the media can novelize health risks (see Brown et al. 1996).

Two Cultures

As mentioned in chapter 2, the media often rely on institutional authorities such as the medical institution to validate their sources. In spite of this dependence, journalists often collide with medical practitioners based on different agendas. Medicine is a science and so differs from other forms of knowledge, such as "common sense" or faith. As a science, medicine is considered positivistic, objective, rational and value-neutral. One major source of conflict between the media and medicine relates to the concerns that the media often portray scientific news inaccurately. In the words of Loseke (2003: 45): "Media present science on the front stage to general audiences and this can be far from the backstage claims scientists make among themselves." Seale (2002) qualifies the conflict between science and the media as "two cultures." He states that tensions ensue between scientists and journalists, because the latter often "oversimplify, extrematise and therefore distort the true nature of scientific research and the content of scientific findings" (Seale 2002: 52). The reasons for inaccurate representations of science by the media, according to Seale (2002), lie in broader social, political and economic structures, including capitalism, patriarchy and medical influence.

Contrary to Hall et al.'s (1978) assertion that representatives of key societal institutions are the "primary definers" of problems for the media, Miller (1999) posits that there are often definitional struggles between institutions and the media. Part of what drives the media interest is news value, such as journalistic focus on violence, scandals and conflicts. This suggests that an official source may not be prioritized by the media if it lacks news value. Singer (1990), in an empirical study, focuses on the inaccurate reports of scientific research in print and electronic media. She indicates that inaccuracies result from the media's need to dramatize scientific findings — they "serve to heighten the dramatic impact of a science report" (Singer 1990: 111).

To state that the media misrepresent or distort science is to assert a perfectly "objective science," which is unmediated by common sense. Miller (1999) posits that under social, political and economic pressures, scientists can maintain positions that depart from strict scientific rules of objectivity. This lends credence to the view that what is considered as science or scientific knowledge may not necessarily be objective. Using the case of bovine spongiform encephalopathy (BSE) in Britain in the 1980s as a focus, Miller (1999) explains how British government officials influenced scientists attached to state organizations such as the Ministry of Agriculture, Fisheries and Food (MAFF) to restrict the definitions of BSE to an animal/veterinary health issue, rather than conceiving it as a potential public health issue. The emphasis in Miller's work is on the process of arriving at scientific findings about risk, most especially the role played by exogenous social forces in the construction of what is risky versus what is not. This process encompasses the vested interests of scientists and government officials: "The privileging of the contingency of science as an explanation directs our attention away from the political and economic contexts in which scientists actually work and which also contribute to the specific ways in which science is communicated" (Miller 1999: 1252).

Nevertheless, regardless of antimonies between the two professions, medical doctors still assume a status of "medical aristocracy" not only because journalists more often than not depend on them as a credible source of information but also because medical practitioners are held in a high esteem by the public. For example, Lupton and Mclean (1998) found in their study of the Australian press that medical doctors and the medical practice still enjoy a significant amount of social authority in spite of negative publicity in the media.

Two major aspects of the media coverage that highlight these differing interests are the source of Ebola as the diagnosis and the disclosure of the patient's name.

The Source of the Word "Ebola"

For the medical establishment and the public the word "Ebola" incurs imageries of awe, devastation and high morbidity. The word is key to the coverage of the incident by the media, and it might have contributed to the high level of panic that the news generated (see appendices 1 and 2). It is around this word that other key issues, such as immigration, insecurity and public health, are framed. Ebola is frightening not only to Canadians, but also to the Congolese. Also, for the Congolese who participated in this study, their knowledge of Ebola is highly mediated by the media and by word of mouth in the Congo, their home country. In other words, all of those who participated in the study, with the exception of one person, had had no direct experience with Ebola. The association of "Congo" with a stigmatizing disease is interpreted as a collective national stigma by the Congolese. For Blacks in the sample, Ebola is stigmatizing and its appearance in newspaper headlines in connection with an immigrant from a Black African country was taken to be stigmatizing as well.

Did the word "Ebola" come from the medical establishment or did the media "fabricate" it? This question is relevant to the understanding of the conflicts between the "two cultures." In *Managing a Mystery Virus*, Jeff Vallentin, the director of media communications for Henderson Hospital, states: "Although we were careful not to use it, within minutes the word Ebola found its way into the airwaves and homes of Canadians. We knew a tidal wave of demand for information and interviews wasn't far off" (Vallentin 2002: 5). One of the medical doctors interviewed claims that it emanated from the media searching for the sensational:

> The word Ebola came through the media. I mean we never said this is Ebola. We thought really that the viral hemorrhagic fever was a possibility and there's a number of viral hemorrhagic fever[s]. The word Ebola was mainly stressed by the media, we didn't really feel that Ebola was the most likely viral hemorrhagic [fever] that this woman would have had anyway.

When the doctor was asked if the word "Ebola" came from the hospital or from elsewhere, the same doctor replied:

> So, when the expert saw the patient, he or she suspected that it could be one of the hemorrhagic fevers. There could have been a long list of explanations for this. Within one category was a list of viral hemorrhagic fevers, so it wasn't that "oh yes, this is a viral hemorrhagic fever, for sure"; they don't know. This could have been bacteria or it could be this, but it also could be this, and because it could be this, we need to take precautions for this, as well.

Although the hospital might have been careful about its use of words, it implicitly assumed "Ebola." In fact, one of the medical doctors interviewed attributed the source of the word "Ebola" to one of the infectious diseases experts. Further, he felt the hospital over-reacted:

> I mean personally, this case should never have gotten into the press, I think it was ridiculous that, you know, there are people coming from Africa much more frequently and other cities like you know, Berlin, London, Paris, and yet Hamilton has this one case that gets all around the world, it should never have been called to the press. I don't think she had [Ebola], she clearly didn't have Ebola, it was probably overcalled and it should never have been phoned to the press.

A journalist mentions that the hospital confirmed the possibility of "Ebola" at the press conference:

> I think what happened was nobody used the word, but the question was asked if Ebola was on your suspect list, and the answer was affirmative. That was pretty clear, and that was pretty clear from the word go. In fact when [a journalist from the *Globe and Mail*] called me and I talked to him, I said did you ask the question outright? Did somebody ask it outright? He said yes, here's the quote, and he replayed the tape for me. I mean so it was pretty clear they may not have been using the words, but when somebody said are you leaving up Ebola, and they said yes, that's on our list.

The word "Ebola" seems like the proverbial hot potato, which no one wants to carry. As indicated in the journal publication by Loeb et al. (2003), Ebola is included in the "differential diagnosis" and it was suspected because of the patient's travel history. But it was the media that had capitalized on it in their coverage. As the previous chapter shows, it was the representation of the disease in a sensational way and the constraining of other possibilities that had a remarkable impact on the readership and the public in general.

Members of the Black community who participated in the study do not exonerate the medical establishment from the source of the word "Ebola." One member of the Congolese community, a non-practising medical doctor, comments:

> If they took Ebola, it was because it was suggested. They said it was [five] diagnoses: Ebola, Crimean-Congo, Lassa fever, Rift Valley fever, yellow fever. All the mention that she was bleeding from different sites was due to a lack of communication. When they were taking the history of this lady, they should have known that she was bleeding because of the needles; that is, the place where they were trying to get the blood. So you can see (showing the newspaper), so when I heard these diagnoses, there was no [mention of] malaria.

Another non-practising Congolese medical doctor comments:

> Even in the Congo, you can't throw something in the media as a doctor, you can't throw something in the door, just throw it because it crossed your mind. I mean even if you come to me with a flu, in my head it won't be flu only. If there are many, there is what we call "differential diagnosis" in our mind. So Ebola was one of the diagnoses. As doctors they should think, but they make it as if it was the only one — the only one they could think of — you see, and with the high tech that I thought that the Canadian medical staff used before coming to a diagnosis, I could never believe that they throw it in a media just the time it was still crossing their mind; the time they were still working on "differential diagnosis."

Interestingly, the Congolese, like other members of the community, relied on the media for their information about the case, so the information they rely on for blaming the medical establishment might have been already compromised.

Naming

By medical ethical standards, persons with contagious diseases may not be publicly identified by the hospital. By the same token, names of people with contagious diseases are hardly printed in the media, especially if they do not pose any threat to the public. Media and medical establishments differ on the amount and nature of information about the patient to be made public. For legal and ethical reasons, the hospital does not reveal the personal information of its patients. On the contrary, journalists believe that good journalism requires paying attention to these types of details.

As mentioned in the last chapter, the identity of the patient is central to the Othering of the disease and for establishing feelings of "we" versus "them." The interview with Jeff Vallentin reveals the media quest for the identity of the patient from the beginning:

> I specifically dealt with our spokespeople to say that we have an obligation to protect her identity as much as possible, to the point of not even revealing whether our patient is male or female. Well, reporters are pretty clever, and the first question from the floor at the first news conference was "doctor can you tell me if she is still alive, or if she's still conscious?" And of course, when a physician answered "no she's not conscious," now they know she's female. So you know pretty tricky! We were careful not to reveal her identity, her name, but it wasn't long before her name was made known through the media.

In high profile health cases, it is not unusual for physicians or representatives of medical institutions to violate patients' confidentiality in the course of informing the public, via the media, about health risks. In a high-profile HIV contact tracing investigation covered by the Australian press in 1994, for example, Brown et al. (1996) show how the hospital can unnecessarily reveal details about their patient's private life under media pressure. In the non-Ebola case, the hospital made efforts to protect the identity of the patient. Under the pressure of the media, the hospital revealed more information to the media than they would have in a normal situation. According to Mr. Vallentin, the hospital "gave specific information about her condition, about her symptoms, about some possible diagnoses that we suspected; about how she was being managed and cared for, in terms of managing the risk of the infection issues."

Regarding the disclosure of the patient's name, Mr. Vallentin expresses his frustration thus:

> Reading from the papers was very disturbing because we were working so hard to protect her as much as we could, and there was a time when we were worried that there was someone at the hospital who had leaked that information, and that's very much against the hospital's values, the way we protect all patients' right to privacy. That was very disturbing. I have to tell you I went through this entire process never knowing her name.

It is evident that the hospital revealed some personal information, given the panic the case had generated, but the disclosure of the name did not come from it. One of the journalists interviewed confirmed that the source of the name was a journalist who had contacted the baggage handler at the airport for the manifest of airline passengers.

As mentioned in chapter 3, disclosing the identity of the patient is not fortuitous. The disclosure is an Othering mechanism. Isaac (1975) notes that two of the most important elements of "basic group identity" are the "body" and "name." The body is the physical and the most essential characteristic of a person. As Hall (1996) claims, the body can be read like a text. In the non-Ebola case, the body encompasses the race, nationality or ethnicity: it is a visible marker of group identity. That is, it is the body that associates an individual with other members of his/her ethnic/racial group. In a similar vein, the name does not only give a person his/her individuality or uniqueness, it links the individual to a group or a national identity. *Ipso facto*, the naming of the patient is central to her construction as the Other — African, immigrant, woman and Black. Naming and shaming are complementary in media representations of crime and may precipitate vigilantism (see Critcher 2002).

Ordinary Voices

Throughout the hospitalization of the patient, the Congolese community maintained that the patient was suffering from malaria, and not Ebola, based on two reasons. First, based on Congolese knowledge of Ebola outbreaks in the Congo, where it only breaks out in rural areas, they deduced that the patient would not have been suffering from it because she lived in Kinshasa, a city of about five million people. The Congolese forcefully asserted that an isolated single incident of Ebola was very rare. Second, since malaria is rampant in Africa, the Congolese interviewees argued that it should have been given a high priority in the doctors' "differential diagnosis." They explained that the transition from the tropics to an extreme Canadian winter worsened the patient's existing medical condition of malaria. A doctor of Congolese descent in the community explains:

> So my reaction was that I refused to accept from the start that it was a case of Ebola virus, and there is an incubation period, and that if she was a genuine case we should have got many other cases with it in Kinshasa, in which case my colleagues [in Kinshasa] should have told me this, all of them professors at the university, and [one] professor was among the experts involved in the first outbreak in Congo.

This interviewee is a trained medical doctor connected with the McMaster medical school. He insists on malaria based on his findings from the patient's personal physician. He further explains:

> Prior to her departure on Friday, she was put on a malaria drug, anti-malaria on Thursday. I heard it from her personal doctor on Wednesday evening I was interviewed [by the media]. Wednesday evening when I called the Congo, the people were angry; they were not happy with the news, because there was no such a case from the tropics where she came, where she flew. When I called I was told she had malaria, and

she was taking a course for malaria which might have been interrupted during the flight.

From the start, he was unconvinced that the patient had the Ebola virus: "so from the start that was my reaction, that it was a wrong diagnosis, wrong label, so there was no such other concomitant outbreak in Congo, there was no such case. And then she was coming from the Congo." In the words of one of the non-practising medical doctors in the community:

> As I said before you don't have somebody who comes with Ebola pre-senting with the symptoms that lady presented. That couldn't be Ebola, because she didn't have any other generalized bleeding. No subcutane-ous bleeding, nothing, no bleeding through the ears, no bleeding through the eyes (opens his eye lids with his fingers to demonstrate to me)… you bleed from everywhere! Every hole you bleed, from the nose, from the eyes, from the mouth, from the ears, you bleed. And when they examine you, if they see that even subcutaneous, you're bleeding, sub-conjunctival bleeding, right? Sub-mucosa bleeding.

Another non-practising medical doctor also "diagnoses" malaria, but also accounts for the bleeding:

> It's cerebral malaria. Here she had a menstruation. Ebola makes people bleed. The nickname of Ebola is hemorrhagic fever so you bleed when you have Ebola. You have diarrhea and all that, so it happened that this lady was having her menstruation, she had a fever, they label it, Ebola! So the head diagnosis was cerebral malaria, and she was treated for malaria, and she was healed. She was treated effectively for malaria.

Like many other members of the Congolese community interviewed for the study, the last interviewee attributed the blood found in her to "menstruation." These voices are not documented in the newspaper coverage. The emphasis is on Ebola or diseases that are deadlier than malaria.

Lay members of the community also have an interpretation. Science is not only subject to review among scientists; laypersons have continuously doubted science, and still do now, more than ever. While discourse produces knowledge that regulates the conducts of others (see Foucault, 1980), Persson et al. (2003) show that laypersons contest the dominance of biomedicine with their experiential knowledge. As Lupton (1999: 75) explains, the imprecise measure of risk has made the public become more critical of science. In her own words:

> The reflexive organization of knowledge environments requires the constant prediction of the nature of outcomes in the future, or risk assessment. This assessment, by its very nature, is always imprecise,

for these calculations rely upon abstract knowledge systems which are subject to contestation and change. As a result, people have become increasingly cynical about the claims to progress offered by traditional modernity.

Wynne (1996) also argues that laypersons, based on their direct experience with natural ecology, have an expertise in the interpretation of natural phenomena. Laypersons or non-experts also doubt and contest scientific knowledge. Wynne (1996) maintains that laypeople do not automatically assume expert competence and infallibility, rather they question expert authority. On the basis of their experiential knowledge of Ebola in the Congo, ordinary members of the Congolese community, like their physicians and those from the Black community who participated in the study, disagree with the official position that was portrayed in the media.

Lay Congolese consistently maintain that it was malaria and not Ebola or any of the hemorrhagic fevers. When one of them was probed on how sure he was that it was malaria, he responds:

> Yeah, we're (laughing) about [it], because we know it's malaria. Malaria can kill you if you are not careful. We know that [it was malaria], all of us have suffered from it, anyone out of Congo must have suffered from malaria at least once at some point, okay? But we know that if you take the medicine, there would be no problem. But if you don't take the medicine, you can die. We got the confirmation from Kinshasa that this lady was sick of malaria, we confirmed that and we said yes it's malaria this is the manifestation for malaria. Yeah, malaria is a very, very serious disease. And when it attacks people could think you're mad. You will start to talk like somebody who's crazy. It's very, very serious. You know that, you're African [referring to me — the researcher].

Even though in the end there was no medical diagnosis (see Loeb et al. 2003), the Congolese strongly believed that the patient suffered from malaria and responded to malaria medication, which "healed" her.

Another Congolese states:

> She was tired from Congo, when she took the airplane. They said she should eat something. When they arrived in Hamilton, the lady [the "hostess"] asked if she could cook something for her. She said no, I can't eat, I'm not feeling well. She was taking medication for malaria. She did not complete the dosage. She made a mistake, she stopped [taking her medication]. That's why she became sick again on the plane. She did not finish the medication. The very night they came to Hamilton, she became sick. The lady [the "hostess"] said "you have to go to the hospital. If you die, I'll be held responsible." When they went to the hospital, she had a menstruation, she was not feeling well. This

> is a woman, she came from the Congo, she had blood everywhere, this is Ebola, they said.

These respondents do not need to be told the difference between Ebola and malaria. They were sure that the patient had malaria. Their reliance on experience is congruent to Persson et al.'s (2003) point that laypersons negotiate scientific-medical diagnoses with their lived experience.

Their responses also corroborate Kitzinger's (1998a, b) study of the relationship between the media and their audience. Kitzinger (1998a, b) argues that people make sense of media discourse in relation to what is familiar to them. Apart from the Congolese scepticism of the medical diagnosis, they also give more credibility to information from members of their community.

Voices, Representation and Power

Alternative media create a space for counteracting the dominant ideology. Through the alternative media, opposing views to official viewpoints are expressed (see McRobbie 1994; Knight 1998a, 1998b; Hier 2002a). The distribution of quoted sources in the four newspapers is an indicator of power differentials among news actors in the coverage. It is not unreasonable that quoted sources in the four newspapers cluster around official actors (doctors, government officials, union leaders and hospital staff) (see appendix). Compared to other groups and organizations, doctors are quoted more often by journalists. This is not unusual. As Stallings (1990) points out, the media often rely on experts in particular fields. Thus, doctors as sources represent 66.7 percent (Ebola period) and 35.3 percent (post-Ebola period) in the *National Post*; 54.8 percent (Ebola period) and 40.3 percent (post-Ebola period) in the *Hamilton Spectator*; 63.2 percent (Ebola period) and 46.7 percent (post-Ebola period) in the *Globe and Mail*; and 46.3 percent (Ebola period) and 57.1 percent (post-Ebola period) for the *Toronto Star*.

The *Hamilton Spectator* and the *Toronto Star* attribute more voice to members of the Black/Congolese community in Hamilton during both the Ebola period and post-Ebola period than the *National Post*, while the *Globe and Mail* has no quotes from Blacks (see appendix). The *Hamilton Spectator* gives Blacks 3.2 percent (Ebola period) and 18.1 percent (post-Ebola period), compared to 11.8 percent (post-Ebola period) of the *National Post*, and 2.4 percent (Ebola period) and 14.3 percent (post-Ebola period) for the *Toronto Star* (see appendix).

The high number of source quotes attributed to the Congolese/Black community in the *Hamilton Spectator* does not translate into their agency. For example, the Congolese doctor connected with McMaster University's medical school was reported in the coverage by the *Hamilton Spectator* and the *Toronto Star* as attributing the patient's illness to malaria. Apart from not being represented in the coverage as a member of the medical community of the university, but as a "Congolese-born radiologist," his perspective is also framed as being in a weak position relative to other physicians of the medical institution who provided a pro-Ebola stance in the media. On only two occasions is he quoted by the *Hamilton Spectator* and the *Toronto Star*; in a few instances he is paraphrased. One of the few statements attributed to him focuses on his critiques of the diagnosis: "'When someone is on such a long trip, changing jets, and this kind of time, you end up with a situation of tremendous bodily stress,' said Dr. Eli Tumba Tshibwabwa" (*Toronto Star* February 8, 2001c). His voice in this media passage can be seen as evasive or unclear as it does not clarify his position on what the cause of the patient's illness is.

In a related instance, and without specifically quoting the radiologist in the February 10, 2001, news item, the *Hamilton Spectator* writes:

> Congolese-born radiologist Dr. Eli Tuma Tshibwabwa, who has lived in Hamilton for five years, sounded a note of concern. He said nobody from the hospital contacted physicians in Hamilton's Congolese community for their advice, even though they've had first-hand experience in the Congo dealing with viral hemorrhagic fever. (*Hamilton Spectator* February 10, 2001f)

The above quote can be read in multiple ways. First, it lends him extra authority because he is Congolese with "first-hand experience" of the disease; and second, he is "a Congolese-born radiologist," a specialist with a non-expert credential, being a "radiologist." Thus his identity is ambiguous and he occupies a contradictory position, which may undermine his authority in speaking on the issue in the public realm.

Samuel Kalonji, who is quoted twice by the *National Post* and the *Toronto Star*, is of Congolese background like Tshibwabwa but, unlike Tshibwabwa, he is not affiliated to a medical institution because he is a non-practising medical doctor based in Hamilton. Like many Congolese community members of Hamilton, Kalonji doubted the early suspicion of Ebola, and, like Tshibwabwa, his insight as a trained medical doctor who is familiar with tropical diseases lacks substance in the coverage: "She had a headache, no appetite, she was confused... they called the ambulance for her and went to the emergency ward with them" (*Toronto Star* February 9, 2001b). There is no tone of expertise in this statement. Nor do they quote him discussing anything related to his medical expertise. He is simply quoted as giving an overview of events.

As pointed out earlier in the chapter, the Congolese community members, including the medical doctors within the community, insist that the patient exhibited symptoms that are consistent with malaria. Malaria is not given much attention in the coverage. The word "malaria" appears less than either "Ebola" or "hemorrhagic fevers" in the coverage (see appendix). The newspapers suggest that malaria could never have been the cause of her illness. For example, the *Hamilton Spectator* is cynical of the Congolese community members' insistence that it is malaria and not something more serious: "The men gathered in Lufuma-Manuel's shop are not doctors, but all insist she is likely suffering from malaria" (February 12, 2001a).

The reliance of the media on institutions for credibility and the de-legitimation of lay knowledge is also evident in the following interview statements made by journalists in connection with malaria as a competing diagnosis:

> The university tropical disease expert they had involved said quite clearly earlier on, no it is not malaria. They denied it, they said earlier on that's not the case. And that's what the [Congolese] community feels, that it's malaria. But I don't know which is right. I don't think the community is necessarily right at all. I mean that's the best guess I have, but I don't think they have any better knowledge than I have. They have some broader experience, but few of them know the real facts other than what was reported in the papers about this. So they are not in possession of better facts to apply to their experience, to come up with a better answer.

In a similar vein, another journalist responds to the question of why malaria was not a consideration in the newspaper coverage:

> In terms of whether the diagnosis was malaria or Ebola, we took our lead from the medical experts. The medical experts can be wrong, but the judgement we made was that because the medical experts were worrying that that was a possibility, and the consequences of that were so serious, that it would be wrong not to tell the community that that was a possibility. We were told by medical experts in Hamilton that they feared that this is what is going on, and our first and last instinct is to inform as quickly as we can the community of what possibilities are. For no other reason, that would allow the community to do what the community thinks it should do. I have the right to know if there is a catastrophic disease in my community or if the medical experts fear there is one. If they are wrong, they are wrong, but if they are right, I should be in a position to do something to protect my health.

What is interesting from these journalists' responses is that malaria was a possibility, among others, but was not given any attention. In other words, the only real possibilities that get recognized are the worst ones.

On February 26, 2001, the *Hamilton Spectator* has coverage on the patient's hostess. She is quoted as follows:

> My life is destroyed. I was looking around my apartment for some-

thing to use. I was thinking I would stop my life. I know Ebola — it will kill you. People stop their own life…my life to this time is destroyed. Everyone is going to know, is going to say, "Oh! That is the woman who brought Ebola to Canada." (*Hamilton Spectator* February 26, 2001)

This depiction of her seems to illustrate a helpless and powerless woman, overwhelmed with emotion, fear and insecurity. However, this overly emotional and sensationalized representation of the woman lacks any other details about her. This contrasts with the impressions that some members of the Black community have of the woman. Some of them have considered her a "good Samaritan" for taking care of a sick member in the community, and also as an ordinary woman with agency: an immigrant woman who is working and attending college. The *Toronto Star* also quotes one Paul Mukaba, complaining about the association of the Congolese community with the virus: "This has demoralized our community, this suggestion that we brought this disease to Canada, to North America. It is bad for our community" (*Hamilton Spectator* February 12, 2001a). Here the Congolese are represented as hapless "victims."

Drawing on Habermas' (1981) conception of the public sphere, it can be argued that the mass media in modern societies are within the confines of the public sphere debate, where rational-critical dialogue supposedly holds. For Habermas, participants in the public sphere debate are equals, even though it is an exclusionary bourgeois domain, and in this space the most rational opinions prevail. Nancy Fraser (1996) takes Habermas (1981) to task for theorizing a unified public sphere. She argues that in an unequal society (such as Canada), the idea of participatory parity is best achieved not in one but a multiplicity of public spheres. It is amongst multiple publics, not one, that rational critical debate takes place. In Fraser's conception of public sphere, fair and balanced views can only emerge in a differentiated and multi-mediated atmosphere. Alternative media outlets, such as the Internet and ethnic newspapers, should have engaged in a critical dialogue with the mainstream media and flawed the dominant frame (the non-Ebola panic in this case).

Hier (2002a) corroborates Fraser's assertion in his empirical study of youth's resistance to the "crusade" against rave culture and finds that the youth successfully redefined the situation through the alternative media. However, he undermines the advantage that the youth's "cultural capital" (Bourdieu 1984) conferred on them. Cultural capital, including tastes, arts and literature, is often associated with the middle class. While economic capital and cultural capital can overlap, at other times they are at odds. New immigrants and refugees may lack the cultural capital for resistance.

For example, members of the Black community made efforts to redefine the situation by sending a delegation of members of their community, headed by a non-practising medical doctor, to a political rally held by the Liberal Party at the Hamilton Convention Centre. They presented to some politicians that the patient was suffering from malaria and indicated that the publicity given to the case had been devastating to their community.[2] Perhaps, the Congolese might have been taken seriously by the public at large if they had brought the press along when they made their presentation to the Liberal Party officials, as it would then have been another media event on the non-Ebola incident.

The preponderance of media outlets with their openness for diverse views has made it possible for powerless groups to articulate their issues and contest their misrepresentation in the media, but the mainstream media still have a powerful influence on members of Western societies, and their "discourses of domination" (Henry and Tator 2002) have marginalizing human material effects on racial minorities. This is not to attenuate the potential of racial minorities to mobilize on the basis of race to fight the domination that is convincingly honed by Henry and Tator (2002). Racial minorities can fight racialization by inverting it and using racial identity as a resource for mobilization (see Stubblefield 1995).

The absence of alternative views in the media consolidated the hegemony of the dominant discourse, leading to what Habermas (1981) refers to as the colonization of the lifeworld by the system, that is, the colonization of the lifeworld of Blacks by the mainstream media. This colonization of the lifeworld is a manifestation of the structure of inequalities that confronts racial minorities, which has translated into their underrepresentation in key Canadian social institutions (see Henry and Tator 2006). Fraser (1995) also identifies two ideal-type obstacles to "participatory parity" in contemporary society. The first centres around "material maldistribution" in unequal societies and the second concerns "cultural misrecognition" in ethnically diverse societies. According to Fraser (2000: 113), "Misrecognition is neither a psychic deformation nor a free-standing cultural harm but an institutionalized relation of social subordination." Misrecognition is perpetrated through institutions that regulate social interaction. Like misrecognition, maldistribution "constitutes an impediment to parity of participation in social life" (Fraser 2000: 116) when social actors are deprived of economic resources necessary for full participation. In spite of their analytical differences, cultural misrecognition cannot be severed from economic arrangements of society. While being cautious not to reify social identity, like race, Fraser advocates for a version of cultural recognition, which she refers to as the "status model," that is not antinomical to material equalities.

Most members of the Black community interviewed for this study have claimed that their views were misrepresented and underrepresented by the media because of their race. This is particularly obvious when the perspective of a key member of the community connected with McMaster's medical school was partially screened out. According to members of the Black community, a social value attached to his race made him less credible. Li (1998), for example, finds an association between the social value of "race" and the market values of "race." The social value associated with "race," according to Li, has an influence on how the competence of racial minorities in the labour market is assessed. Race might have mattered to journalists and news organizations in their determinations of what is "credible," "believable" or "truthful." However, the misrepresentation of Blacks should not be obfuscated from its social-structural moorings. The demeaning representations of Blacks — cultural injustices — are linked to the underrepresentation of Blacks in key social institutions like the media and medical field. For example, many of the medical doctors of Congolese origin in Hamilton are not practising. Stallings (1990) and Knight (2001) have indicated that there is a relationship between a group's strong attachments to official institutions and the corresponding quoted sources in the media. In this case study, racial categorization and the underrepresentation of Black immigrants in key institutions of society conflate and precipitate the marginalization of their voice.

Notes

The title of this chapter is an expression taken from Berger (1992: 16).

1.   The interviews that appear in this chapter were conducted between February 2003 and October 2003. Nearly all members of the Black community were interviewed in their homes; one medical doctor was interviewed in his home and another was interviewed over the phone; and the director of media communications for Henderson Corporation was interviewed in his office in Hamilton, Ontario.

2.   I could not get any hard evidence to support this. I relied on the information received in the field from more than three members of the Congolese community. The leader of the community, who was helping with documents related to this activism, suddenly, and sadly, passed away three days before our scheduled meeting. Members of his family were not able to trace the documents for me.

Chapter 5

Community Reactions

The last hard news item on the non-Ebola event was featured on March 20, 2001, in the *Toronto Star*, titled "No mandatory insurance." On March 14, 2001, the *Hamilton Spectator*, the *Globe and Mail* and the *National Post* all published their last hard news items regarding the event, titled respectively "Visitor health insurance not likely in Canada"; "Ontarians leave trail of hospital debts, too: Suspected Ebola victim's tab unpaid, but official says residents also fail to pay up"; and "Ontario: Mystery illness bills unpaid." As stressed in the previous chapter, there was under-representation and misrepresentation of Congolese/Blacks' voices in the news coverage. The dominant discourse suppresses alternative and ordinary voices in the media not only because they lack strong institutional connections but also because they are opposed to the dominant frame.

The *Hamilton Spectator* of March 9, 2002 covered a story (with the head-line "Spectator reporter nominated for top newspaper award") about the nomination of one of its journalists for reporting on the non-Ebola scare. The reporter is commended for doing "a terrific job on a specific story" and for bringing "great credit to the newspaper." Yet, very little is presented in the four newspapers examined for this study about how the non-Ebola panic was experienced by members of the Black community. However, much about the feelings of racial minorities to the coverage was made clear in letters to the editor that appeared in the *Hamilton Spectator* of March 20, 2001. The letters to the editor were written for the commemoration of the International Day for the Elimination of Racism, marked on March 21 of every year. The following are excerpts of some of the letters written to the *Hamilton Spectator*:

A letter written by Quan Nguyen reads:

> Did you know that blacks were the most targeted for these move-ments of racism, but there were many others also. An example was a visitor who was thought to have Ebola, and a group of racist people were handling out pamphlets that said, Immigration Can Kill You. It turns out that she did not have it. (*Hamilton Spectator* March 20, 2001)

Miles Anderson writes:

> In fact, in 1997 in the City of Hamilton, numerous hate crimes

were committed, the majority of these were against blacks. I'm sure you've all heard of the Congolese woman who came to Canada with a mysterious illness suspected of being the Ebola virus. Brochures were sent out by the Heritage Front Party containing the message: Immigration Can Kill You. The recent Hamilton Spectator headline, "Sick visitor is our neighbor in the global village," reminds readers that we should show compassion to people, no matter where they are from. (*Hamilton Spectator* March 20, 2001)

Excerpts from a letter by Josh Fortier read:

What is racism? Racism is the belief that one ethnic group, race or religion is superior. The Heritage Front handed out racist leaflets outside Henderson Hospital more than a month ago that stated, Immigration Can Kill You. Anti-racism groups reacted that week by calling on Hamilton Mayor Bob Wade and Police Chief Ken Robertson to protect visible minorities and natives. They want to create a special Anti-Racism Committee. A recent report by the Hamilton Social Planning Council found minority groups believe discrimination exists in the region such that it grows as a person's complexion gets darker. (*Hamilton Spectator* March 20, 2001)

These letters mostly allude to the racialization of Ebola by the Heritage Front. The Heritage Front might have been singled out because its own version of racism is blatant, overt and unpolished (see Barrett 1984, 1987; Li 1995; Hier 2000). The focus on an old-fashioned brand of racism by the media can divert people's attention away from new racism (Barker 1981), which is as pernicious as any other racisms. This chapter presents the perspectives of members of the Black community, the impact of the coverage on members of the community, their resistance and inhibitions to the grassroots Black mobilization and the significance of racial identification to a racialized group's agency. It is evident in the analysis of interviews with non-Congolese Blacks that race consciousness plays a key role in their interpretation and understanding of media coverage and the reaction of the public to the Black population. For analytic convenience, participants in the study are divided into two categories: Congolese and non-Congolese. Nationality appears to be primary to the former, while race is a rallying point for the latter.

Blacks' Perspectives and Interpretations of the Coverage

Members of the local Black community have various explanations for what drove the story. Their perspectives on the high level of attention paid to the case by the media include fear, nationality and the race of the patient.[1]

All the respondents felt that the story was made bigger than it should have been, but they offer different explanations for the amount of attention given to the case. For the respondents, fear is one major factor, but the race and nationality of the patient also drove the story. One non-Congolese Black respondent who was quarantined as a result of his close contact with the patient holds that fear motivated the story:

> Well, if it were true obviously then knowing what Ebola was explained to be, it was an infectious disease that if it went out there it had a tendency to infect many Canadians, and so, you know… it was a health concern, and a big one. So obviously, if you look at the contingent of doctors and medical people and the team that worked around [the patient], you will really know that it was a big concern for the people. I mean it's a big health hazard.

In a similar vein, a Congolese respondent suggests that the story was driven by a public health concern:

> Think about the nurse who came in contact with the victim, and that nurse goes home and she has a husband and kids who go to the day care or school, see how the thing is gonna be. So whoever gonna be coming in contact with those people is exposed to the disease so I think it was a huge public health issue.

A Congolese respondent states:

> Ebola is not like any other disease. This is a serious disease, right? It is a killer! There is no cure for that disease, there is no cure for that disease as we all know if you have Ebola [and] you survive, you have to praise the lord. Yes, because it's a killer disease, so it was that panic which went throughout the Canadian community that if the Ebola comes here to Canada it means people are going to die in big numbers, I think it was that fear which made it to be a very, very big news.

A non-Congolese Black respondent states:

> It was a big story because it was different, people actually started comparing. There is a movie that was made years ago, um, it was the monkeys? Was it about Ebola or something else? People actually started to think. I mean the media carry so much weight, you know, so that was about it. And to make it even worse, it was a Black person, okay, so we don't have to keep anything under wraps.

There are others who hold that race *per se* was the driving factor. One of the respondents, a non-Congolese, explains: "Because they have all the ingredients that people like to hear. They have a Black person, they have a person who they thought was an immigrant. They have a disease that was making headlines, so they combined all these ingredients."

Journalist Laurie Garrett (2000) witnessed and covered the outbreak of the 1996 Ebola outbreak in the Bandundu province of the Congo. From her own account, Ebola generated a generalized state of panic and anxiety among the Congolese. It is then not a surprise that the Congolese feel that Ebola is worth giving public attention and concern, and that it might not necessarily be racist. However, some of the participants have expressed concerns about its representation in the media as a Black disease.

Perception of Racism

Only once was the concept of racism mentioned in the questionnaire presented to respondents during the study. The exact wording of the question was: "Some people have claimed that the media was racist in its coverage, what did you think of this claim?" In most cases, interviewees brought up the concept of "race," "racism" or "racist" and when this happened they were probed for elaboration. Contemporary racism has been differentiated because of its emphasis on culture/nationality, as opposed to a racism articulated around physical differences, such as skin colour. The contemporary form of racism is referred to as the "new racism" or neo-racism (see Barker 1981; Balibar 1991). The new racism shares with the "old racism" a hierarchical ordering of *Homo sapiens*: cultural differences for the new racism and presumed physical differences by the old racism. However, unlike the pseudo-scientific racism, which is more obvious and blatant in expression and practice, the new racism is very ambiguous (see Satzewich 1998a: 218–19) because it is less detectable in conception and execution. As Balibar (1991) explains, the new racism is a "racism without race":

> It is a racism whose dominant theme is not biological heredity but the insurmountability of cultural differences, a racism which, at first sight, does not postulate the superiority of certain groups or peoples in relation to others but "only" the harmfulness of abolishing frontiers, the incompatibility of life-styles and traditions. (Balibar 1991: 21)

Members of the Congolese community are less consensual on their interpretations of what constitutes racist media coverage of the case than non-Congolese Blacks in the sample. In the following sub-sections, I discuss the perspectives of the non-Congolese group followed by those of the Congolese.

Non-Congolese Blacks' Perspectives

Among non-Congolese participants, only one felt the media were not racist, but that the coverage could incite racism:

> I don't know if the media was racist, but I did think it's a sensationalist coverage, and non-stop coverage, in the fact that the coverage after a

while tends to almost seal the decision. I think that could perpetuate some racist tendencies that other people may already have, and especially when you look at the polls about how visitors into Canada should be screened and things like that, and visitors from which country should be screened more than other countries, so I think, I think it allowed itself to, yes, play into racist hands. Although, I'm not sure if the media itself particularly was racist.

However, in another context, the same respondent states that she was offended by the way "immigration" was singled out in the coverage:

I think just coverages that said that immigrants from particular countries should be screened more or the ways in which the immigration itself was put into a bad light, as if the arrival of people itself is just bad in the first place.

The remainder of the participants maintained that the coverage was racist. The following are some of their responses:

I think any time that they kind of have a big divide between people or like it's a media portrayal "us" and "them over there" sort of mentality, then there is always racism somewhere you know around that. And that was definitely the case. "We have never seen this virus, us, experts do not know what is"; "This is a foreign virus, it came from Africa." You know all of this kind of catch phrases and stuff like that, foreign, exotic... it definitely hyped into a kind of racism.

We're all here so some form of sensitivity must go into any form of reporting. No matter how bad it is, as such you have to have proof. Without proof it becomes more devastating because then you have to backtrack and try to do the apologizing which is not necessary if you get your facts straight before you come out, before the media comes out. So the form of insensitivity that was the most racist happened. It was in the paper, people can read it, the wording that was chosen for explaining the situation. [Pause] I still get chills when I talk about this. How could it have gone so far so quickly?

It was very racist, very systematically excluding. Any other piece of information, except what was coming from the mainstream, and picturing the whole continent as a place where you have only diseases.

In my view it is a racist coverage, and it's very discriminatory and dangerous. When you have people writing and they don't have a proper analysis of racism, I think they are filling spots, and their knowledge base...if you are not aware or trained to understand how oppression works, you're gonna write the same view learned and seen.

> The way it was reported made it look like that. It was as if that this person was a Black person was why the issue is very critical, and that if any other nationality, either British or German or whatever, came into the country and fell that sick, chances were, that the attention would not have been the same.

One of the respondents drew on the SARS outbreak and the impact on the Asian population to buttress her point that the coverage was racist:

> I think it was racist. I thought, maybe, you know, it doesn't matter where you came from, especially coming from Central Africa you know, I just thought it is because she came from Congo. Just look at the SARS now, and think about how the Chinese people now are treated. Every Chinese now feel like maybe they have SARS. So people have stopped going to their restaurants, and a lot of people have stopped buying their food. And you know, it is good to alert people, but sometimes it does a lot of damage. It might last long.

These participants have a strong conviction that the patient was treated differently in the media because of her ethnic origin and race. From their perspectives, this special treatment constitutes racism. It is implicit from their expressions that if she had been of European descent, she would have been treated fairly.

The Congolese Perspectives

Members of the Congolese community are more divided when the question was posed to them. A respondent who does not believe the coverage was racist explains why:

> I can't say that it was racism. It's just a lack of information, which led to what made people label it as racist. At my level, in my opinion, I didn't see it as such a racist labelling in that. It's just the fact that she came from out of Canada, from Africa, she was labelled as a case of Ebola virus so the local community would have seen this a potential danger, to the health of the community, and fear might have been interpreted by the Black community as racist, but from my point of view, we can't say that the fear of potential infectious disease can be interpreted in terms of racism.

However, the respondent adds:

> You may have people with such [racist thinking], it's unfortunate with such kind of understanding who may just see that as an opportunity and then they may say "okay, that's Black people who are bringing this disease here." At the end, some may take it with such a racist connotation. In my opinion I saw it differently, but I have to acknowledge it that in this society, people may have different ways of doing this, and of reacting and they may say that's the Blacks who brought it.

Another Congolese responds: "No, I wouldn't jump to that conclusion, not racist because I don't have anything to base my judgment on that." In a similar vein, one member responds to the question as follows:

> People in the community gave it quite a racist note. But my personal feeling is that I don't think that it is a racist note. It's like any new disease, if it comes for the very first time to North America, and it's deadly, they would talk about it, I'm telling you, and in a high note.

Li (2001), in his analysis of racist subtexts in Canadian immigration documents, claims that racism becomes insidious when its discourse is encoded in a neutral way. In a state of new racism, the appearance of inter-racial diversity might occlude a systemic form of racism. The response of the following participant is an example of a person's perception of incompatibility of racism with multiculturalism:

> Oh, I will not say really racist, that I will not say that, but information, they need to do their work and sell newspapers, they need to get information to people. For the racist, I cannot say that, because Canada is a multicultural country and a multi-racial country because in the media we have Black, we have everyone, you know I cannot say it was racist, no, that is not the point, no.

However, a Congolese participant thinks the coverage was racist:

> It was a big issue because the person was Black and she was coming from Congo, and they were looking at immigration itself, like how can someone who is sick get to Canada? She's coming from a high risk country, so putting all together with the colour made it a huge issue. I don't think that would have happened if that was a Canadian who went to Africa and came back bringing Ebola, right? It's just because the person really came from Africa and they think that person has it even though it may be something different. So I think the colour issue was in place too, I don't think they would have done the same with the Canadian who went to Africa for two weeks and came back, I don't think so.

The Congolese responses are not unique. In fact they represent the divisiveness in the Canadian public of what constitutes racism. This is not only because the definitions of racism can be politicized by claims makers (see Miles and Brown, 2003; especially their notion of conceptual inflation and deflation) but also because racism has different components (Kallen 1995: 41–57), which makes the concept problematic.

Public Reactions and Community Impacts

Some members of the Black community experienced stigma from the public. Negative public reactions to health scares often stem from panic. Panics can lead to discrimination against marginal groups (see Power 1995). Some members of the Black community feel stigmatized by members of the larger Hamilton community who distanced themselves in public settings, such as schools and children's playgrounds, where inter-racial interactions often take place. Most encounters of members of the Black community with discrimination (de)generated into what Murray refers to as micro-panics — "interactional processes that occur within local contexts" (Murray 2001: 513).

There is an interesting pattern to research participants' experiences of rejection and stigma associated with the disease. For example, while an average Congolese person would recount how it directly affected him/her or persons that were very close to him/her, such as close friends or relatives, it was not common to find in the sample a non-Congolese Black person claiming a direct effect. One reason for this "difference" may be because Blacks in Hamilton do not tend to cluster in a geographic area of the city, while members of the Congolese community in Hamilton are close because they are relatively small in population and homologous in social strata. Most Congolese in Hamilton are recent immigrants and mostly do non-standard jobs.

The public reaction has a general impact on Blacks in Hamilton for the fact that it was discursively constructed in the media as a racial disease, and it was difficult to distinguish Congolese from non-Congolese (recall in chapter 3 the discussion, analysis and implications of racializing the disease by framing it in a racial way). In the following sub-sections, I discuss the nature of the impact of public reactions to the news of Ebola on members of the Black and Congolese communities in turn.

Impacts on Non-Congolese Blacks

Only one person in this category claims that he was personally affected by the public reaction to the news. Being "personally affected" would entail effects on an individual and close relatives and acquaintances. Nevertheless, all the participants are aware that the news had some impact on Blacks in Hamilton. It is public knowledge in the community that Black children were taunted and segregated in some schools in the Hamilton area. One of the participants in this category who works with a social service agency in Hamilton recalls the encounters of Black students in Francophone elementary schools and in children's playgrounds, based on what she heard from people directly affected:

> I remember a mother who was from Congo and her children in
> Francophone school that the children were coming home crying because

the other children were running away from them, telling them you're bringing [diseases] and that all people from Africa bring diseases to us. We had a large number of Congolese, for a coincidence at that time in Hamilton, which was fairly new to the whole system; and as from the neighbourhoods to the schools, people were harassing. I remember a woman telling me her child was asked to leave a playground in a town house because she would make them sick.

Another participant in the study who works with the City of Hamilton and is active in the community describes the interpersonal encounters of some Black school children with what she calls "racial profiling" in some of Hamilton elementary schools:

I went to several schools, tried to mediate, tried to help some children, and their families, deal with the schools. It was a very difficult timing. In Hamilton we have a good percentage of people of colour; they are located in pockets of the city so some of the schools have more Black children and children of colour than others. Some don't have any at all. So some of the schools that have problems, their Black population was really victimized, and it just became racial profiling that happened in schools, and we tried to help out with that, work with those issues, but then again you know the incident escalated when the Heritage Front groups started picketing, and handling out fliers.

The only person among this group with a close encounter with the patient and her hostess is a community leader, who is also a church priest (will henceforth be referred to as the "community leader"). He was quarantined because he had close contact with the patient at her residence, and when he accompanied her to the hospital. When the hostess fled from her place of residence out of fear of the media and hateful stares from her neighbours, she was accommodated by the community leader. He recounts his experience dealing with her melt down thus:

We have to put up with the lady probably so because that's the profession that I'm in, to help people as a pastor, just that and especially for my wife who had to be with her especially during those times. She would literally break down, weeping and stuff like that, and it was [an] emotional problem. There were stories here and there that some Blacks were being shunned, some Black children being shunned at public school because of the suspicion that they may carry some deadly disease and if they got near to them, they might be transmitted to others.

Most non-Congolese Blacks make reference to the taunting of Black kids in elementary schools by their peers.

Impacts on the Congolese

The public reaction to the news, as recounted by the Congolese, affects individuals and the entire Congolese community. Individuals recount their direct encounters with stigma and rejection based on their association with the patient as Congolese. One of the respondents who just arrived in Canada two months prior to the incident and was enrolled in an adult education course in Hamilton recounts that following the news about a possible Ebola virus in the community, a staff member at the adult education school was scared of sharing his pencil with him. In his own words:

> At that time I was new, quite new in the country, at the adult education centre, I was myself a victim because when I went in the human resource [centre] I couldn't share the pencil with the officer in that centre. That time I remember when I went there, I was looking for a pencil to write something and when I tried to take his pencil, he took it away, he said: "don't touch it I don't... I'm afraid to get sickness." So it's a big concern for us because some kids known as Congolese origin have also been mistreated in school because the people started to be afraid of Congolese people.

The respondent later took part in the founding of a Congolese association in Hamilton and was part of a group that initiated a coalition with other Black organizations.

As Hamilton and Trolier (1986: 133) point out, through interpersonal relations pre-existing stereotypes are confirmed by those who hold stereotypes. Pre-existing racial stereotypes of immigrants as likely carriers of infectious diseases might have confirmed a hypothesis that racial minorities carry diseases. A respondent's children attended a local school that was close to where he lived with his family. With some emotion, he reluctantly responded to the question of how the coverage affected him, his family and people he knew:

> It affected us a lot, a lot, a lot. They got children who are attending schools here, some were subjects of abuse, you know, at school when other children learn that they are from Africa, they start avoiding them. My kids were included. It really had a serious impact on us. Yes, my kids were schooling here, not far from here. They start asking them, even some teachers, "Are you from Congo"? "You have brought Ebola?"

Another Congolese participant claims that his five-year-old son was affected by the spread of the news:

> My son was very affected because in the school, friends were asking him, "Okay, you're from Congo, you have Ebola too." He was very upset, he was asking me if he had Ebola too. People were very upset in the community. Yeah, they were very upset. We got some friends

whose children were in the same school, while traveling on the bus to the school, people were asking "You're from Congo? We want to know about Ebola, you're from Congo?"

As the above quotes show, the public has associated the disease with the Congo and the Congolese. This may not be unrelated to the emphasis placed on the Congo in the news headlines. As earlier indicated, headlines have cognitive impacts on the readership. News headlines, composed of a disease and a nationality, can have ideological effects on those who read the news. They are capable of directing public attention to the Congolese, and also immigrants, as carriers of the disease.

The woman who hosted the patient left her apartment traumatized. She also lost her babysitting job as her employers feared for their health and that of their children. The community leader who accommodated her recounted her condition thus:

> At some point in time because of all the things that had been put into the news media… you need to have an idea of what she went through… she was with us for close to five months, we really had to talk to her. There were times that she was contemplating suicide and all of that because of what the media put out about her, you know. Here's somebody who is a refugee claimant, her papers were not through yet, so the thought of: "What's going to happen to me?"; "it would just jeopardize my application." Also, she had no family here, she was all by herself so she went through an emotional trauma.

Etoroma (1992) has noted that there is an ambiguity around the Black identity: that is, racial identity competes with other social identities among Black Hamiltonians. Because the event is constructed by the media around the Congolese national identity, the Congolese nationality might take precedence over the Black identity. As a group, the Congolese view the coverage as a collective stigma and a negative portrayal of their nationality (see chapter 3 for a thorough analysis of identity and nation). Some members of the Congolese community in the Toronto area and in the province of Quebec phoned members of the Congolese in Hamilton, and some of them came to Hamilton to provide them with support. Given the international attention the case generated, Congolese in Europe and in the U.S. phoned their family members and acquaintances in Hamilton to inquire about the condition of the patient and the reaction of the local community.

The perceived negative portrayal of the Black community precipitated local solidarity among its members. In the next section, I discuss the resistance to the coverage and efforts made by members of the Black community to re-define the situation.

Agency and Competing Perspectives

Discourse does not always succeed in silencing alternative perspectives. As Fiske (2000) points out, dominant discourse does not extinguish competing discourses, even though it may contain them:

> The regime of truth produces, circulates and grants truth-effects to what we might call "official'" knowledge. While repressing and denying truth-effects to other knowledges which we might call situated, or local… but while they may be contained, these situated knowledges are not extinguished, and the containment is never total. (Fiske 2000: 56)

As discussed in previous chapters, one ideological function of the media in their coverage of the incident is to suppress alternative views. By so doing, they screen out the agency of the Black community. In spite of the power of the dominant media to suppress oppositional views, there is always resistance. In the following sub-sections I discuss the Black community's forms of resistance. They range from communal support of the patient, to redefinition, to the formation of an association and to enhanced Black consciousness.

Communal Support

Members of the Congolese community at the time came together as a group to support one another and to complement the institutional bio-medical care that was provided to the patient. As discussed in chapter 4, the Congolese insisted that the Ebola virus was not responsible for the patient's illness. They followed this up by contacting the patient's medical doctor in the Congo and getting a confirmation from a specialist, Professor Tamfum Muyembe — a world-renowned expert on Ebola (see Garrett 2000: 50–120). According to the Congolese, the information they received from the specialist in the Congo was passed on to the treating team, recommending that the patient be treated for malaria.

In local Congolese churches in Hamilton, prayers were said for the quick recovery of the patient. A priest in the community visited the patient in the hospital to pray for her quick recovery. The Congolese community also sent a delegation to the hospital to meet with the patient, to pray and to provide her with social and emotional support. Members of the Congolese community met regularly in the house of one of their leaders in Hamilton to express their concerns about the negative impact of the coverage and to discuss ways to deal with the negative impact they believed was generated by the media. One Congolese describes the main goals of their meetings thus:

> We held meetings as Congolese people with friends, Congolese from Toronto. We held meetings and we tried to find out how we can counter-

attack and how we can assist the young lady in hospital, and also how we can find out or inform Hamilton politicians.

The agenda of the Congolese includes care for the patient, counteracting the dominant frame in the media and politicizing the case in order to expose media misrepresentation.

Redefining the Situation

Members of the Black community made efforts to redefine the situation. The Congolese sent a delegation of members of their community, headed by a non-practising medical doctor, to a political rally held by the Liberal Party at the Hamilton Convention Centre. At the rally they argued that the patient was suffering from malaria and indicated that the publicity given to the case had been devastating to their community.[2]

The Black community leader met some local journalists in the company of the patient's hostess on two occasions. An interview they granted a *Hamilton Spectator* journalist was published in the *Hamilton Spectator* of February 26, 2001. The community leader and the hostess negotiated and managed to protect her personal information, including her name and photograph, which the journalist requested. The objective of the first interview is described by the community leader as follows:

> We were trying to tell her story rather than the media portraying her as somebody who is harbouring… and she's the person for all this confusion is about. It was made to look like this girl had come from Congo to literally spread the Ebola disease that would kill everybody in Canada or something, that was what she was made to feel like. She has hosted somebody who's become a medical risk to the country. So when I finally kind of got a hold of her to go, our hope was that we were gonna straighten up the issue and tell the story as to what is going on for her, to solicit sympathies from the public rather than the continuous barragement and harassment from the media. So we granted the guy the interview. At the end of the day, what was published was a little skewed.

Due to their dissatisfaction with the way the media "skewed" the story, the community leader and the hostess decided not to grant further interviews to journalists. He states:

> It [the media] didn't really portray what we intended to tell to solicit the sympathy of the public so that's when we said that we not gonna talk to no more person, but a lady from the *National Post* in Toronto called me here several times, and wanted to make an appointment, I said no. CH (a television station) wanted to come and talk to me, I said no, I don't wanna talk to nobody. I declined no more of that because it looked like they were not interested to tell our side of the story, they were just look-

ing for information to feed what their suspicions were. I wasn't gonna
go into all that.

The second interview was an initiative of the community leader. After
the patient was discharged from hospital and the news story about Ebola
dropped, the community leader went to the *Hamilton Spectator*'s office to grant
the newspaper an interview for the purpose of persuading the journalists to
write a story portraying the hostess in a positive light. According to him, the
Ebola story had had devastating effects on the hostess such that she could
not function normally in the community without ridding her association with
the non-Ebola crisis:

> I actually went to the *Hamilton Spectator* office to talk to them, trying
> to get them to appreciate what they had done to her, and the fact that
> because of that she doesn't even have a place to stay, and that now
> that the Ebola thing is over if they could create some public awareness
> and get some well-meaning individuals within the public to help resettle
> her and rehabilitate her, at least emotionally and they couldn't bother
> so much about that.

The newspaper granted an interview with the community leader but did not
publish the story because the journalist who conducted the interview was con-
vinced that the government would not grant the community leader's request
for the hostess's rehabilitation. The community leader had the conviction
that the media could positively influence the woman's life.

Formation of the Congolese Association

The non-Ebola crisis had a positive side effect in having reconstructed
the Congolese community. Conflicts are not necessarily a disadvantage in
ethno-racial relations. According to Cashmore (1990), conflicts signify a
development of a sense of belonging by immigrant groups. Conflicts may
be involved in the process of immigrants' claims of rights. An awareness of
rights by immigrant groups may mean that they are adapting to their new
society. Conversely, acquiescence to perceived oppression and inaction may
mean that an ethnic group is not aware of its rights or lacks self-confidence.
In situations where marginalized ethnic groups fight for their rights, they are
affirming that they belong.

Coser (1956) points out that "social conflict" may "contribute to the
maintenance of group boundaries and prevent the withdrawal of members
from a group" (Coser 1956: 8). Although the incident did not lead to a collective grassroots Black mobilization for various reasons discussed later in
the chapter, it indeed led to the birth of the Congolese association, Amitie
Canado-Congolaise (ACC — Canadian Congolese Friendship). Immigrants
derive social and psychological empowerment from voluntary associations.

Many voluntary organizations command greater participation, enthusiasm and personal commitment than those in which activities are done for pay (Sorenson 1990: 313) because they provide racial minorities with ontological security. Borrowing Giddens' (1990, 1991) terms of "dis-embedded" and "re-embedded" social relations as an analogy, migration "dis-embeds" immigrants from their local moorings, family and friends, while voluntary associations "re-embed" them in their new country by integrating members into their new society and linking them with co-nationals in both host and home countries (see Goldring 1998).

The experience of the Congolese with the non-Ebola incident motivated members of the community to found an association that would protect their collective interest. Lupton and Tulloch (2001) empirically explore Beck's (1992) notion of risk in late modernity by focusing on cross-border stories and narratives of immigrants and migrants in Australia. Aside from environmental and health risks, other risks, such as conflicts and warfare, exist for immigrants, migrants or border crossers. Contrary to Beck's grand theorizing of late modernity's transition from distribution of "goods" to that of "risks," Lupton and Tulloch (2001) find that insufficient "goods" or lack of them is still a major source of anxiety for some immigrants. Other sources of anxiety for immigrants and refugees in late modernity are violence in their home country and loss of intimacy and contact with family members left behind. It is evident that the non-Ebola incident gave the Congolese an impetus to form an association to confront other pre-existing problems. The secretary of the association, who had not arrived in Canada at the time of the incident, describes the objective of the association as follows:

> The Ebola disease motivated us. Without the disease, there wouldn't have been a motivation. They did not have an organization that they could use to express themselves. There was no unity. The organization was created to fight for their cause. Ebola was the major reason.

The Congolese have looked at the non-Ebola incident from a positive angle. As explained by one of them, the incident provided an opportunity for Congolese unity:

> It was because of that incident that we say: "eh guys we shouldn't submit like this, we must build a community, [a] Congolese community in Hamilton." As such if something happened we should stand up and talk about it. That is what made it possible, and we had a well-organized community in Hamilton because of that. If it was not for that we were not going to build it. Even in our meeting, when we see that lady we said: "God, thanks it's because of you that we've built this."

The chief objective of the association was the maintenance of group solidarity for the purpose of resisting related incidents in the future. They are also making a coalition arrangement with other Black associations in Hamilton. One founding member explains the efforts being made towards a coalition of Black organizations and the objectives of such a coalition:

> We are trying to set up a committee of African people with the help of one of the organizations here to try to bring the Black community together. [So] those who are living here in Hamilton see exactly what are our problems, the common problems [are] and try to address them. We are in the process of setting up a committee. We have already had one meeting and one of the problems raised will be that problem of Ebola.

Further, he says:

> We're more concerned about Black people. Because we don't have the same problem as Arab people; we are African Blacks. Ebola will be one of our concerns, work discrimination, any kind of discrimination — problems we are having, so we've got all those types of problems and [will] try to see exactly what we can do because we are in the process of going to meet the local authority.

One can infer from the above quote that "racial conflict" is not necessarily disadvantageous. Apart from leading to group cohesion, it enables those who suffer from racial oppression to address other systemic issues, such as unemployment, and to demand institutional reforms (see Cashmore 1990).

A local Hamilton organization called the Community Coalition Against Racism (CCAR), which is made up of members of different ethno-racial groups committed to anti-racism, considered the coverage by the media anti-immigrant and racist. They met on a number of occasions to discuss ways to address the damage that the incident was doing to the Black minority ethno-racial group in Hamilton. The head of the organization, Ken Stone, is quoted in the *Hamilton Spectator* of February 22, 2001, advocating for the rights of racial minorities. In the same article, there are reactions to the presence of members of the Heritage Front and their leafleting of hate crime literature in the neighbourhoods around the hospital. There are appeals to the city council administration to create an anti-racism committee that is separate from equity organizations dealing with sexism and homophobia.

Factors that Undermined Collective Black Mobilization

Etoroma (1992: 289) identifies external and internal factors underlying the "relatively weak social organization of Blacks in Hamilton." Internal factors are a lack of effective Black leadership, fragmentation along cultural and nationality lines within the Black population and the ambiguity of Black identity. The external constraints to community building are racism and stigmatization. These factors — external and internal — undermine community building but do not imply absence of a Black community; for, Etoroma (1992) notes, these inhibitions to community building are neutralized by community efforts at building a unified Black community that undermines those differences. The notion of a community among Black Hamiltonians is built around the idea of "race," through what Etoroma calls "intra-group interaction" (Etoroma 1992: 300). Intra-group relations among Blacks in Hamilton often take place through voluntary organizations, including Black churches, national associations, social service associations, fraternal organizations and businesses. In addition, the growing perception of Canada as home by Caribbean and African immigrants who have adapted to Canada also facilitates interaction among Blacks in Hamilton and enhances Black cohesion.

This study reveals the fragmented nature of the Black community in Hamilton. In a sense, the relatively modest amount of resistance to the perceived negative coverage came from the Congolese. It was mainly the Congolese in the sample who explicated the intricacies of the case. Except for one member of the Black community (the community leader), all members of the non-Congolese group interviewed, as well as members of the larger Black community spoken with informally, knew little about the patient's personal details and knew very little about her specific health condition.

Fragmentation and Absence of Black Leadership

In situations of uneven power distribution, the dominant group is able to use the media to assume "ideological closure" (see van Dijk 1993a). Effective counter-discourse depends on organization and articulate presentation of counter-definitions by a sub-dominant group. To this, Hall et al. (1978) state as follows:

> Primary definers, acting in or through the media, would find it difficult to establish a complete closure around a definition of a controversial issue in, say, industrial relations without having to deal with an alternative definition generated by spokesmen [sic] for the trade unions, since the unions are now a recognized part of the system of institutionalized bargaining in the industrial field, possess an articulate view of their situation and interests, and have *won* "legitimacy" in the terrain where economic conflict and consensus are debated and negotiated. Many emergent counter-definers, however, have no access to the defining process at all. (Hall et al. 1978: 64, emphasis original)

Hall et al. (1978) have also indicated that fragmented groups have difficulty mobilizing against primary definers: "the closure of the topic around its initial definition is far easier to achieve against groups which are fragmented, relatively inarticulate.... Any of these characteristics make it easier for the privileged definers to label them freely, and to refuse to take their counter-definitions into account" (Hall et al. 1978: 65). In the case of the non-Ebola scare, lack of leadership and fragmentation of the Black community undermined collective resistance to what a segment of its membership perceived as racially motivated negative publicity. However, a lack of effective leadership and fragmentation of community do not imply an absence of community.

According to Etoroma (1992), early in the history of Hamilton Blacks, the church and its leadership were a unifying factor for the Black community in Hamilton. Subsequent growth and ethnic plurality of the Black population in Hamilton have de-centred the church from Blacks' socio-political life. The declining role of the church as a unifying force in Black Hamiltonians' lives can be inferred from the community leader's experience:

> When I had granted an interview, you know, to Bill or Humphrey [a journalist with one of the newspapers], one of the church members saw my name in the national papers and cautiously warned me not to go into the media because once you start with the media, you never know where they would take you to, you might have good intentions of wanting to disclose information but only heaven knows, they would start digging you, surveillance on you and all of that and so your life gets sparked with all this media attention.

Further, it is evident from the community leader's account of events that the individual interests of some members of the church mitigate collective action:

> A cross section of the church members were concerned that, you know media as it is, you never know what they would put up; you know even if you grant them interviews, so a cross section of the church members who had businesses were concerned that if I got too much into the media, one of these days they might want to target the church and some of the individual businessmen in the church so they kind of advise me to stay out of it.

The hesitation of some members of the community to contest their negative portrayal in the media is a pragmatic approach based on their calculation of the damage that media attention could further do to their community. The community leader adds:

> See, I didn't want to spearhead that because I didn't want to seem very political. I was hoping that the people within the Congolese community would take that up, and if they needed support, but not to spearhead it. I knew the community or Congolese community came together a couple

of times. They were thinking of legal action and all of that, but to an extent they pulled out. There was another Congolese pastor who ended up taking [the patient] when she was finally released.

The experience of the community leader *vis-à-vis* his church members throws light on the receding political influence of the church in the lives of Black Hamiltonians.

In addition to a lack of leadership and fragmentation, the Black community is also described by some members of the community as apathetic and acquiescent to domination. Even people who claim to be leaders have a tendency to essentialize the Black community by failing to recognize the diversity within it. In explaining why Blacks did not mobilize to contest the negative media coverage, a leader in the community claims that in addition to a lack of respect for leadership by Blacks, economic subsistence is more important to Blacks than political mobilization. In her own words:

We did not come together in a mass. We did not demand that there were retractions done. We did not. We did not take the kind of political step we should have taken, because we do not have anyone speaking on our behalf. A lot of us working in the community give a lot of ourselves. I have given twenty-five plus years, but there are some, even within our community, who would say, "Well she is not talking for me." Who the hell am I talking for? And that is what is happening within our community. They are afraid of speaking out, because they have to put bread on the table, and they have to keep a roof over the head, and that's serious business. The children have to be in the school, they don't want them to be railroaded so they take it. And they encourage the children to take it so the circle continues. One of these days we will wake up. We will.

In relation to Africans, another member of the community who is of Congolese origin laments their apathetic attitude toward claiming their rights:

We Africans, we don't have the culture of fighting for what we believe in; that is part of our culture. We don't really fight for our right, for what we believe in, when we are discriminated against, we don't really fight, that is part of our culture. I'd rather say it is blindness.

This Congolese respondent's claim that Africans don't fight for their rights is inconsistent with the fact that some members of the community made an effort to redefine the event. Lack of unity among Blacks in Hamilton, as well as individual interests and apathy, as expressed by the above participants, however, mitigate against collective Black mobilization.

Cultural Capital and Recency of the Congolese

Literature has recognized the alternative media as a space for expressing alternative viewpoints, that is, voices that are not associated with official and powerful institutions in society (see McRobbie 1994; Knight 1998a; Hier 2002a). Alternative perspectives represent the voices of "ordinary people." McLaughlin (2001) has conceived of marginality and intellectual innovation in relation to cultural capital. Two of McLaughlin's (2001) four ideal types — optimal and sub-optimal marginality — are applicable to the situation of Blacks *vis-à-vis* their degree of resistance to the dominant frame of the non-Ebola panic (McLaughlin 2001: 273). McLaughlin (2001) claims that there are relationships between marginality and creativity. While innovations can emerge on the margins, McLaughlin (2001) argues that innovations from sub-optimally marginal intellectuals can be rendered futile because they "have inadequate economic, cultural, institutional, network, and personal resources to carve out unique and powerful innovations in dialogue with centrally located intellectual traditions" (McLaughlin 2001: 273). Apart from insufficient material resources — or lack of them — for this set of intellectuals to challenge orthodoxy, they also lack the cultural and emotional capital to challenge orthodox establishments. Non-affiliated or non-practising Black doctors in Hamilton have ideas, but their scarcity of material, social and emotional resources make them incapable of successfully challenging the medical orthodoxy. So, the ideas are in competition, but the lack of resources and opportunities affect Blacks' ideational success in the context of the competition over the definition of the symptoms. The concept of "sub-optimal marginality" also applies to the entire Congolese community, which was in the process of establishing itself in a Canadian city.

McLaughlin (2001) also argues that intellectual change and the transformation of ideas are more likely in a condition of "optimal marginality" because optimally marginal thinkers are in possession of alternative sources of resources to sustain their ideas. Hier's (2002a) study of rave culture, for example, shows ways that members of the rave community contest the discursive construction of raving as a potential health risk. Although in the concluding part of the study Hier (2002a) recognizes the importance of social class and ethno-racial backgrounds of members of the rave communities to their effective subversion of dominant discourse, he leaves this out in the substantive part of his work. Members of the rave communities thus fall into the "optimally marginal" ideal type (McLaughlin 2001). Late modern societies are highly mediatized. Social agents, in their struggles for hegemony, politicize issues in the media (see Fairclough 1998). The media, including the Internet, in late modern societies are used increasingly to publicize oppositions to dominant institutions' construction of health and risks (see Gillett 2007). It is the Congolese lack of cultural capital, in the sense of negotiating their political stance in their meeting with the Liberal Party, for example, not knowing to involve the media as a conduit for bringing their cause to public attention, which kept the public unaware of opposing angles to the story. In the course of collecting data for the study, I spoke with people of diverse ethno-racial backgrounds outside of the Black community in Hamilton and Toronto. While most of them were aware of the incident, they did not know how the case was closed. Most people did not know that the diagnosis of Ebola was hotly contested, with malaria forcefully expressed by the Congolese as an alternative diagnosis.

Studies have shown that new immigrants, by virtue of their vulnerability, build institutional networks for their protection against domination by established ethnic groups and dominant institutions (Breton 1964; Chavez 1994; Tilly 1997). In the case of the Congolese, their newness seems to have undermined effective resistance. Most new Congolese immigrants in Hamilton were refugee claimants and were marginally employed at the time of the incident. As refugee claimants, they were vulnerable and avoided activities that they felt could jeopardize their chances of staying in Canada. Most immigrants from Africa have a strong attachment to their family members and the community. Family members depend on them for material well-being through remittances. Studies in the area of transnationalism have documented the importance of immigrants to the economic survival of their home countries (see Smith and Guarnizo 1998). The Congolese, like other immigrants in their situation, would have to be extra-cautious in their dealings with the media and avoid publicity or anything that can jeopardize their chances in Canada because family members in home countries count on their financial and material support. In conversation, one of the journalists interviewed expressed his frustration regarding the difficulty he encountered in retrieving information from members of the community. He complained that they avoided giving information and, when some of them did, they refused to provide personal information about themselves that could be used to legitimize media sources. He added that Canada was a free country where everyone was treated equally and that the Congolese should have nothing to fear. The fact is that members of immigrant communities never take the regularization of their immigration status lightly. The newness of these immigrants and the tenuous immigration situation of many Congolese are some of the structural factors inhibiting immigrants' integration into their new society. Structural inequalities deny some racial minority groups access to the media. As van Dijk (1993a) holds, access to communication is one of the indices of power in our modern society.

Racism and "Self-Inflicted Alienation"

In his dialogue regarding Manoni's (1964) conception of Blacks' "dependency complex" as natural, Fanon (1967) attributes Manoni's notion of this dependency complex to the racial oppression of Blacks. Racism, Fanon (1967) argues, leads to self-alienation. Racism widens the already existing social distance between Self and Other. Racialized members of society begin to view themselves as not belonging to the society that they are actually a part of. Li (2003) has stressed that people with discernable physical features are racialized when they are by default presumed to be "immigrants" (see Li, 2003a: 44-45). Basch et al. (1994) have shown that racial minorities concur with their racialization and internalize their Otherness. Tones of non-belonging and Otherness are detected in the voices of some members of the Congolese community. Some of them view racism as "natural" and "inevitable." Some also see themselves as "strangers" and view biased journalism as professional. An example of a self-alienating response to a question by one of the Congolese respondents follows:

> That happens for all countries not just Canada. If you are a stranger, you are a stranger, okay? If she was really Canadian, things can be a little bit different, because for Canadians, Canada is the pure country, and sickness can just come from outside of Canada.

In another instance, a Congolese individual believed the coverage was racist but noted that: "It's racist, 'racism' is natural too. It is the first reaction for everybody to an outsider." A sense of being a "stranger" and an "outsider" is symptomatic of immigrants accepting their construction as non-Canadian (Li 2003). It is also a sign of a diminished relationship between the Self and Other, which can translate into apathy. Nevertheless, some other members of the community, most especially non-Congolese Blacks, provide a systematic explanation of racism. Their analysis relates to Giddens' notion of how "sociological thinking" is inter-penetrating the lay audience who has come to interpret the world sociologically. In Giddens' words, the lay audience is "thoroughly sociologised" (Giddens 1990: 43). To this end, some members of the Black community have analyzed the Ebola case as a consequence of racial intolerance in Canada. A respondent analyzes the phenomenon of racism as societal:

> When things of that nature happen people find a way to express their racism full force and it's like... I'll go back to the burning of the Samash Temple after 9/11, and even things that happened after 9/11, that kind of stuff, you know racism is something that is not in-born, racism is a learned behaviour, so it comes out in full force, and people feel they can express themselves as they feel at that time because it's everywhere so it's not me alone.

Some of them view the suspicion of Ebola in a Black person as providing the opportunity for some members of the public to express their hatred or condescension toward racial minorities. The sense of "not belonging" to Canada by the Congolese partly contributed to their reluctance to publicly dispute the media claim. The sense of "self-alienation" exhibited by some immigrants is a reflection of the folkloric conception (Li 2003) of refugees and immigrants as "outsiders" in their "host society."

"Immaturation" of the Panic

Mainstream sociological studies of moral panics conceive of panics as a disproportional reaction of the public to what it perceives as a threat to its collective interest (Cohen 1972; Goode and Ben-Yehuda 1994). The moral panic literature does not deny the existence of a problem but doubts the ideological content that recruits the public's reaction to a panic. In the case of the "mods" and "rockers" in Britain in the late 1960s (Cohen 1972), there were some concerns around perceived moral and cultural shifts in British society. The public perceived the behaviour of some groups of youth as "real" problems that warranted collective action. More than before, "folk devils" have had more options for fighting back (McRobbie 1994). In the case of non-Ebola, it was a mis-diagnosed and a wrongly suspected disease that came to an abrupt end as soon as the error was detected. The discovery of the absence of Ebola led to an abrupt termination of the coverage and resultant public reaction. This makes the anti-immigration discourse difficult to sustain over time. The abrupt end of the panic does not give one a chance to witness how events would have unfolded had Ebola been discovered. However, one can speculate that a positive diagnosis of Ebola would have been a potential risk given that a handful of people in the community would have been exposed to the virus. Anti-Congolese and anti-immigrant sentiments would have thus emerged as a reaction. There was also the possibility that counter-claims makers from the anti-racism community would have emerged. The SARS case is an example of how the maturation of a moral panic can lead to an opposition by the subaltern group to neutralize dominant definitions (see Gillett 2007).

Agency, Racial Consciousness and Resistance

Howard-Hassmann (1999) criticizes "race essentialism" (see Jhappan 1996). Focusing on the persistence of "primordial" ethnic identities among immigrant groups in Canada, Howard-Hassmann (1999: 526) argues that "illiberal multiculturalism" is based on a primordial understanding of identity that "categorizes people and obliges them to live within those categories." In other words, illiberal multiculturalism emphasizes generalizations about a group over the individual. While Howard-Hassmann (1999) asserts that identification with ancestral ethnic groups can be reactionary in the Canadian context of multiculturalism, other studies have argued that the persistence of ethnic particularism in modern societies is not necessarily reactionary, but progressive (see Satzewich 1998b: 34-35; Miles and Brown 2003: 91).

Ethno-racial particularism, expressed in a primordial form, can serve as a bulwark against racial oppression, or as a way of contesting patterns of structural ethno-racial inequality. Racial orderings in the U.S. are articulated by the American state in its differential incorporation of immigrants in its social policy (Nagel 1994) and, by implication, a hegemonic construction of America as a country of "Whites." (See Satzewich 1991, for the Canadian version of a "differential incorporation" of immigrants through the immigration policy.) In effect, racism and racial categorizations become evident in the larger society, including its major social institutions. Contrary to the view that the invention of ethnicity or race by the sub-dominant groups is retrogressive, ethnic particularism is agentive. Olzak (1983) has shown that it is easier to mobilize a group on the basis of ethnicity or race than class. In other words, "race essentialism" can be progressive if it provides an impetus for fighting real and perceived oppression by sub-dominant ethno-racial groups. Frankenberg (1993) refers to this way of fighting racial oppression as "race cognizance." Unlike "race essentialism," which divides people into a hierarchical order based on assumed physical differences, "race cognizance" occurs on the terrain of battles against racism and neo-racism.

Stubblefield (1995) distinguishes racial identification by members of the racialized community from biologically construed essentialism. Stubblefield (1995) argues that the difference between an essentialist racial identification and a non-essentialist one is the process of labeling individuals as a category and the connotation of the label. Accordingly, labels totalize differences, stereotype, disrespect and put a burden on people to whom labels are applied. In essence, racial categorization is a particular form of labeling that has disadvantageous effects on the labelled people. She explains:

> The fact that a particular label has been applied to a person makes a significant difference in that person's life. It has affected her interaction with other people in particular ways, and it has determined the label-specific social norms with which she has had to contend. People who live in the same society (and in some cases in the same world) and have been labeled in the same way may not have other experiences in common, but they have had to cope with the same label and the same norms. (Stubblefield 1995: 361)

Of importance to Stubblefield's (1995) point is the "justification" for racial identification, for to differentiate a "non-essentialist" racial identification from an essentialist one, there must be a basis for the identification in the first place. She asserts:

People who are experiencing oppression on the basis of the same label are justified in feeling connected to each other in a way that they may not feel connected to people to whom that label does not apply: although they cannot assume that they have had the same experiences with social norms and assumptions based on the label they share, they do know that the same norms and assumptions apply to them. (Stubblefield 1995: 364)

Although the media did not attribute the Ebola virus to Blacks, members of the Black community identified with anti-immigrant subtexts in the media narratives and related with the plights of the patient and the Congolese because of their association with them as part of a marginalized racial group. The attachment to the patient on the basis of "race" is of significance. The following statement by a respondent of Caribbean descent reveals the phenomenal/emotional import of race for Blacks:

> That should have never happened, never, and I hope it never happens to anybody, especially somebody from my *community*. I hope it never happens again, absolutely because it was too frightening, too devastating, for too many people, and it still is, and they suffer in silence, like Black people are so used to. If something happens to a Black person in the community, it happens to me, I am part of that person. I mean if something happens to human beings, it happens to me, because I'm a human being also, I feel. *But when it comes to my own community like everybody else, we feel deeper, and I mean [the patient] is my sister by association*, by culture, so it did hurt me.

From the perspective of the above speaker, skin colour has a strong emotional importance for her association with the patient. The emotional attachment to race by Blacks is in congruence with Goffman's (1963: 20) explanation for why persons in a similar "stigma condition" bond:

> The first set of sympathetic others is of course those who share his [sic] stigma. Knowing from their own experience what it is like to have this particular stigma, some of them can provide the individual with instruction in the tricks of the trade and with a circle of lament to which he [sic] can withdraw for moral support and for the comfort of feeling at home, at ease, accepted as a person who really is like any other normal person.

As Etoroma (1992) observes, Blacks in Hamilton (as elsewhere) differ in terms of social class, occupation, education and nationality. Skin colour is what Blacks share in common. Skin colour is also a label loaded with social meanings. It is the categorization of Blacks that impels their self-recognition as a group.

As has been discussed, the Congolese community in this sample is more divided in their interpretation of the media coverage of the incident as racist than the non-Congolese community. This is in spite of the direct effect of the coverage on the Congolese population. Interestingly, the incident has not left the entire Black community with a negative impression of Canadian society. One would have thought that the Congolese would view Canada as a socially hostile place for immigrants. Contrary to this, nearly all the Congolese in the sample consider themselves fortunate to be living in Canada, a land of opportunities. Conversely, all the non-Congolese participants view Canada as a discriminatory, exclusionary and racist society. Interestingly enough, I did not see any significant difference in the material conditions of both communities in my observation and knowledge of them, albeit the sample by no means represents the Black population in Hamilton. Given their relatively similar human-material conditions, how could one account for their different inter-subjective interpretations of racism and Canadian society? The only qualitative difference is the length of stay in Canada. The non-Congolese, on average, have been in Canada longer than the Congolese: three of them came with their parents at a young age; two came as adults in the 1970s; two in the early 1990s; one in the late 1980s; and one is a descendant of African-Canadians whose family tree in the Hamilton area dates back to the nineteenth century. Conversely, the Congolese in the sample came in the 1990s and 2000s.

Most of the non-Congolese people interviewed claimed that they had experienced discrimination in different ways. They mentioned their struggles with discrimination at workplaces and in schools. This may have accounted for their negative perception of Canadian society and its major institutions. Concerning the Congolese, their positive impression of Canadian society might have to do with the popular belief that Canadians do not express racism as overtly as their neighbours to the south, which may mean that the Congolese have not lived in Canada long enough to recognize the subtleties of racist stereotypes in Canada. If this has some sociological sense, it then means that it is a matter of time before the Congolese would "assimilate" with other Blacks in perceiving Canada in a similar way. However, this study is not able to cogently provide an explanation for the difference in patterns of perceptions within this Black population. Instead, the study prioritizes other interests, namely those surrounding the media coverage and the impacts on the Black community. Before one can conclude that the relatively recent arrival of the Congolese to Hamilton has some influence in their relatively high positive impression of Canadian society, given their experience with the non-Ebola case, studies are needed to empirically examine the directionality of immigrants' perception of Canada over time.

In this chapter the perspectives and interpretations of the non-Ebola case by the Black community in Hamilton have been discussed. The spontaneous incidence of rejection, such as the exclusion of Canadian children of African descent in schools experienced by some members of the Black community, is a search on the part of dominant group Canadians for certitude in a time of ambiguity, which is analogous to Beck's metaphoric expression "how neighbors become Jews" (Beck 1998). Contemporary Canadian society is confronted by ambivalence when they also struggle to reconcile "race" with citizenship and immigration with social problems. It is evident that ethno-cultural differences within the Black community are attenuated by their acquiescence to racial categorization as an agentive measure. Blacks' construction of their identity around race differs from a biological conception of race in the sense that it is a reaction to their racialization in the media and the way some members of the public reacted to them as a category. Racial identification provides for Blacks a feeling of ontological security in their insecure, alienating social world. The different ways in which the Congolese and Blacks resisted the construction of their being dangerous to Canadian society are discussed. However, it has been stressed that strong opposition to the negative construction of Blacks by the media coverage was undermined by the fragmented nature of the Black community, the lack of leadership, the recency of Congolese immigration, the abrupt termination of the panic before it reached maturation and the absence of cultural capital among the Congolese, who were more directly affected.

Notes

1. The interviews that appear in this chapter were conducted between April 2003 and October 2003. Most members of the Black community were interviewed in their homes.
2. As mentioned in chapter 4, I could not get any hard evidence to corroborate this point. I relied on the information received in the field from more than three members of the Congolese community. The leader of the community, who was helping with documents related to these events, suddenly passed away during the collection of the data.

Chapter 6

Towards a Denouement

Sociologist Peter Berger (1992: 14) describes "sociological consciousness" as a way of looking beyond the "façade of social structures." Sociological consciousness is not averse to the study of mainstream society, but takes into account the perspectives of the voiceless in society. According to Berger:

> The sociological frame of reference, with its built-in procedure of looking for levels of reality other than those given in the official interpretations of society, carries with a logical imperative to *unmask the pretensions* and the propaganda by which men [sic] cloak their actions with each other. (Berger 1992: 14; emphasis original)

If this book accomplishes anything, it is that it goes beyond the official/public definition of the non-Ebola event, looking at it from multiple perspectives. It examines the perspectives of individuals who played varying roles in the case, including physicians, journalists and members of the local Black community, and analyzes the contents of four of the newspapers that covered the story. It is evident that the non-Ebola story, like most novel ones, is a "media event" (Fiske 1996: 2) because of the role played by the media in amplifying what turned out to be an obviously innocuous situation to cause insecurity and set an anti-immigrant tone. This chapter summarizes the book, and proffers "institutional inclusiveness" as a panacea to media misrepresentation of racial minorities.

Most members of the Black community interviewed for the study and most of those spoken with informally claimed that the negative publicity given to the coverage was racially motivated. There was no reference to the patient's gender and class position. The possible role that the class location of most members of the Black community played in making the media narrative effective was not part of how members of the community made sense of the situation. With respect to gender, it is important to know that the woman was attended to by White male physicians. There was no significant presence of female physicians/medical experts in the diagnosis process. Nor was there any female presence from the medical community in the press conferences convened by the hospital. Her situation was also used to reinforce the ideology that women of colour are dependent and overburden Canada's social programs (Thobani 2000). The patient became a medical and public curiosity as African women often are historically (see Gilman 1985). The public awareness of her medical condition through the mass media fulfilled the vicarious fantasy of a society who already had certain impressions of Africa and African women just like Hottentot Venus satisfied the curiosity of Europeans in the nineteenth century (see Hall 1997).

Nevertheless, a different type of immigrant that Miles and Satzewich (1990) refer to as a "postmodern capitalist" may not fit into the same negative stereotypes as the Congolese visitor. Postmodern capitalists include "various categories of managerial, technical and professional staff" of transnational corporations, who are able to circulate in different parts of the world where their transnational corporations have subsidiaries (Miles and Satzewich 1990: 343). Many postmodern capitalists are non-Europeans from the economic semi-periphery of the world. For a postmodern immigrant, the issue of high medical costs would have been muted in media discourse, and the photographing of the "seedy neighbourhood" she stayed in would have been unnecessary. As Ma and Hildebrandt's (1993: 486) study shows, early media coverage of the Chinese in the 1970s focused on culture but, over a period of some ten years, the discourse shifted from "dirty Chinese" to capitalist competitors. They state: "As a group moves from the margins to societal mainstream, coverage is less likely to focus on the exotic and unusual, both because the group is seen as less exotic and because it is more involved in mainstream activities." The improved human-material condition of socially and economically disadvantaged groups is a step toward greater respect for racial diversity and racial equality (see Oriola and Adeyanju 2009). As well, social and economic integration of racial minorities advances us toward racial equality. As long as new immigrants and racial minorities remain disadvantaged economically (see Galabuzi 2006), incidents such as stereotyping and anti-immigrant sentiments as in the non-Ebola case will persist. All in all, this case was not all about race, but a complex articulation of race, class and gender. Race/immigration duality appeared to be the meta-narrative, and for Black observers, race was recognized as their master status in Canadian society.

Beck (1992: 75) qualifies the risk society as a "scapegoat society." Risk is easily displaced to other spheres of life in the risk society. Social change in the form of globalization is a major feature of contemporary life, and, with it, racial diversity has also accelerated. In the context of Canadian society, growing racial diversity is one great source of anxiety for members of a society that has been historically constructed in ethno-racial terms, that is, as an extension of White Europe. Therefore Canadians have always had a "racial capacity" (Barrett 1994: 270). Anxieties have mounted in recent years over the growing number of new immigrants from the "non-traditional societies" of Africa and Asia in Canada (see Zong 1994; Simmons 1998a;

Li 2001, 2003). It is also noted that anxieties over racial diversity are not peculiar to Canada but are also present in other Western societies such as Austria (see Wodak and Matouschek 1993), the Netherlands, Britain and Germany (see Husbands 1994). Some members of the Canadian public have come to view the presence of non-White immigrants as an anathema and a challenge to Euro-Canadian hegemony (see Hier and Greenberg 2002). As has been argued in this book, the non-Ebola event provides a space for the media to tap into the ambiguity of nationality and race as well as the generalized socio-cultural strain experienced by many Canadians. The media do not impose the dominant ideology because Canadians, like other human beings, are capable of classifying people into racial categories. They have what Barrett (1994: 269) qualifies as "the inherent classificatory propensity of the human mind."

The cross-articulation of immigration with contagious diseases is a mode employed by the media to recruit the public to identify with their discourse of difference. Through problematization, complexly related, differentiated issues such as health care and global risks are consolidated in a meta-narrative of immigration. To problematize is to enlist the intervention of social control agencies in policies and practices involving health care, security and immigration. In other words, the media articulation of health risks with immigration was not a fortuitous exercise; it was meant to appeal to social institutional authorities for social control. The problematization of immigration, as discussed in chapter 3, is a call for border control agents to avert an occurrence of similar events in the future, that is, to avoid an apocalyptic vision of tragic immigration. The non-Ebola event is problematized through the articulation of immigration with health and social welfare and the disarticulation of the event from medical error and the advantages of immigration to globalizing Canadian capital. The dominant discourse of risk in the media berates alternative, competing discourses. The dominant discourse stresses spatial control and regulation but screens out public health in the developing countries. The discourse is silent on preventative measures of working in conjunction with developing countries to stamp out virulent viruses that might pose a threat to humanity. The media discourse favours a control model and excludes development discourse. It is a discourse of spatial control that is represented in the form of territorial invasion. It is a discourse of social distance, the distancing of Self from Other. It is a discourse of expurgation of the Other. The logic of social control is articulated in the discourse of moral panic and risk. Risk and moral panic discourse becomes a discourse of apocalypse in the way the media indicated that non-Ebola this time is predictive of its future imminence. This is expressed in the editorial expression "there will be a next time."

Risk and panic discourses are always about the future. This is why the media have the potential to call for the intervention of social control agents. Risk and panic discourses are ideological in that they tap into humans' existing feelings of insecurity. In the media representation of the non-Ebola event, the patient symbolically epitomizes future risk as it is unfolding today. There are concerns about what "she" is going to do in the future—a subtext for what immigration is going to do in the future. In this sense, "immigration" is a coded word for the presence of racial minorities in Canada. The logic of risk and panic discourses is a logic of social control (Cohen 1972; Hall et al. 1978; Dew 1999). The immediate urgency is to contain "them" now or to control "immigration" now before it becomes totally destructive to "us." It was the same discourse of the Chinese Other with diseases that was espoused in the media during the SARS outbreak shortly after the non-Ebola incident in 2001. As with Ebola, race and immigration became a proxy for risk.

Content analysis of four major newspapers and semi-structured interviews with journalists, physicians and members of the Black community were used to collect data for the study. The limitations of content analysis relate to its inability to address issues about the social process involved in the running of the non-Ebola story and capture the inter-subjective experiences of physicians, journalists and members of the Black community regarding the non-Ebola case. The semi-structured interview approach addressed aspects of the research that content analysis was not able to fully capture. Interviews with journalists, physicians and members of the local Black community provided complementary information and an additional understanding of the event, most especially the experiences of individuals involved in the case.

People's interpretation of media texts can differ along racial lines. For example, people can be divided along racial lines on the appreciation of media coverage of an infectious disease like AIDS (see Kitzinger 1998b). However, this study found that there are no undifferentiated views on media coverage of health within a racial group. In this study, there was a diversity of meanings within the Black community. That is, Blacks do not hold the same views on issues pertaining to the media coverage of the non-Ebola event. Their interpretation largely differs along immigration history. For example, non-Congolese, who had lived in Canada longer than the Congolese in the sample, were more disposed to viewing the coverage as racist.

All members of the Black community interviewed for this study had considered the media coverage of the non-Ebola case as a negative portrayal of the Black community. Interestingly, however, the incident has not left the entire Black community with a negative impression of Canadian society. One would have thought that the Congolese would view Canada as a socially inhospitable place to live, considering that the public reaction affected them more than other Blacks. Contrary to this, most of the Congolese who participated in the study consider Canada a land of opportunities and a safe place to live. Conversely, the non-Congolese Blacks interviewed view Canada as a discriminatory and racist society.

Media and Social Inclusion

van Dijk's (1993b) insights on the underlying structural cause of the reproduction of ethno-racial inequalities by the media in modern societies are instructive to the understanding of the racial dimension of the coverage of the non-Ebola scare. van Dijk (1993b: 244-247) states that hiring, newsgathering and social cognition are integral to the reproduction of racism by the media. According to van Dijk (1993b), the overwhelming majority of journalists in the mainstream media are White, and they view issues through their cultural lens: most of them have a superficial and poor knowledge of minorities. In the specific Canadian context, there are very few racial minority journalists working in mainstream newsrooms (see Henry and Tator 2002; Tokunbo 2006: 348–351).

In the case of newsgathering, van Dijk (1993b) indicates that White journalists, who have dominated the media institution, are likely socialized in the dominant culture, whose values they have internalized. Not only this, they have access to dominant institutions in society, whose staff share similar norms and values with them. Thus, the process of reproducing the perspectives of the dominant group in society is complex and is driven by "prevailing social structures, everyday rules and routines, and fundamental social cognitions" (van Dijk 1993b: 246); but the individual White journalist cannot be held responsible for his/her prejudice.

The literature on the mass media and racism has held that ethno-racial power differentials in society are accountable for negative portrayals of racial minorities (van Dijk 1993a, 1993b; Henry and Tator 2002). Negative portrayals of racial minorities by the media perpetuate and maintain existing inequalities among ethno-racial groups. Reduction in ethno-racial inequalities would translate into reduction in negative portrayals of racial minorities. Institutional inclusion of racial minorities would enhance their participation in major institutions, which means that they would have more say in institutional policies and practices.

Kallen (1995) has pointed out that social distance reinforces ethnic stereotypes in the sense that "insiders" relate to "outsiders" in terms of their preconceived assumptions rather than viewing them as individuals. Inter-ethnic interactions attenuate social distance and make individuals increasingly aware of their similarities, rather than their differences. Kallen (1995) also believes that education without association would not reduce social distance and stereotypes. Social distance will be reduced with interaction between different ethno-racial groups (Kallen 1995: 48). The educational and professional training of journalists cannot reduce racial and ethnic stereotypes and social distance. Indeed, journalists who covered and wrote the non-Ebola story were educated. Ethno-racial interaction may not eliminate racist stereotypes and racism, but it may reduce them.

Fleras and Elliot (2003) propose institutional inclusiveness as a solution to the misrepresentation and under-representation of racial minorities in the media. They conceive of institutional inclusiveness as "institutional accommodation" that "involves a process by which institutions incorporate diversity by adjusting institutional design, operation, and outcomes to make them more 'minority-friendly'" (Fleras and Elliot 2003: 312). Fleras and Elliot (2003) are positive that "multiculturalizing" mass media institutions in Canada would entail institutional inclusiveness. In response to an increase in hate crimes in Hamilton following the crisis of September 11, 2001, Strengthening Hamilton's Community Initiative (SHCI) was founded. SHCI was a community-based project that aimed toward the inclusion of Aboriginals and racial minorities in key Hamilton institutions. Its central objective was educating the public about diversity as well as improving the material conditions of ethnic, racial and religious minorities, Aboriginals and women by giving prominence to their participation in the community's major institutions. Toward this end, the community-based project intended to bridge the cultural gaps among members of the diverse Hamilton community. The local newspaper, the *Hamilton Spectator*, was one of the participants in this community-based project. By participating, it was anticipated that the newspaper could be more responsive and sensitive to minority issues and racial diversity.

Diversifying the media's workforce and openness to viewpoints of diverse members of the Hamilton community is a positive step towards a reduction in ethnic, racial and cultural stereotyping. Insensitive and inadequate understandings of Other-defined groups like Africans played a role in the negative coverage of the non-Ebola panic. This was evident in my encounter with one of the journalists interviewed, who covered the story for the local newspaper. The journalist thought that some Congolese individuals were uncooperative in telling the newspaper their own side of the story. He did mention that when they provided information, they wanted their anonymity guaranteed. In a way, the Congolese struck the journalist as a group that had something to hide, or to borrow Pratt and Valverde's (2002) expression, the Congolese struck the journalist as "masters of confusion." I suggested to the journalist that the Congolese might be uncomfortable if they were concerned about their immigration status in Canada. The journalist retorted and insisted that the Congolese should not have anything to fear in Canada and maintained that, unlike the Democratic Republic of Congo, Canadian law treated everyone equally and protected all regardless of their immigration status or cultural backgrounds. This journalist had good intentions, but he looked at the situation exclusively from his own personal perspective. The withdrawal of some members of the Congolese community, as observed by the journalist, was similar to the situation of Arabs and Muslims following the attacks on the World Trade Centre and the Pentagon and the downing of United Flight 93 on September 11, 2001 (see Bahdi 2003), even though the non-Ebola scare was a short lived experience for members of the Black community. As with Arabs and Muslims after 9/11, fear, anxiety and humiliation ensued in the Black community because everyone was considered a risk to Canadian society. Had the media incorporated diversity into their policy and were journalists tolerant of other cultures, the insensitive representation of a racial group in the coverage of the non-Ebola panic would have been averted.

Medical and media institutions traded blame (see chapter 4). Agents of the two institutions exonerated themselves from the negative portrayal of the Black community. The media blamed the hospital for suggesting Ebola; while the hospital blamed the media for choosing the worst of the possible diagnoses it suggested. They can continue to blame each other, but certainly the author cannot be separated from the text. That is, both the journalists and the physicians were constituted by the discourse of the Other that had permeated their intersubjective lifeworlds. The media relied on the medical institution for much of their information, and not on members of the Black community. The hospital might claim that it had been misrepresented by the media, but they needed the media to express their concerns about what they considered "extraordinary." All the social actors of both institutions have certain perceptions of the African Other through socialization. Apart from the exclusionary nature of these dominant institutions, individuals who work within them assume subject positions that are informed by the apparatuses of socialization, including the media, the education system, the judiciary and the family. As for the public, the news that an African visitor or immigrant was carrying a deadly exotic disease would never be doubted because it confirmed their pre-existing knowledge of the African Other. On the whole, the non-Ebola incident was emblematic of a bigger ethno-racial inequality in Canadian society.

Appendix

Frequency of Key Words in the Media Coverage

Themes	Key Words	National Post		Hamilton Spectator		Globe and Mail		Toronto Star	
		N_1 (%)	N_2 (%)	N_1 (%)	N_2 (%)	N_1 (%)	N_2 (%)	N_1 (%)	N_2 (%)
Diseases	Ebola	20(39.2)	16 (16.5)	55 (28.1)	76 (15.4)	25 (26.6)	11 (10.4)	37(21.9)	35(26.7)
	Malaria	0(0.0)	1(1.0)	6(3.1)	13 (2.6)	1(1.1)	3(2.8)	7(4.1)	3(2.3)
	Hemorrhagic fevers	3(5.9)	2(2.1)	23(11.7)	46 (9.3)	10(10.6)	6(5.7)	20(11.8)	9(6.9)
	Meningitis	3(5.9)	1(1.0)	8(4.1)	5 (1.0)	1(1.1)	0(0.0)	2(1.2)	0(0.0)
	Lassa	2(3.9)	0(0.0)	7(3.6)	7 (1.4)	1(1.1)	0(0.0)	8(4.7)	2(1.5)
	Marburg	2(3.9)	0(0.0)	4(2.0)	5 (1.0)	2(2.1)	2(1.9)	3(1.8)	5(3.8)
	Crimean-Congo	1(2.0)	1(1.0)	5(2.6)	9 (1.8)	4(4.3)	0(0.0)	6(3.6)	3(2.3)
Panic	Deadly	5(9.8)	5(5.2)	16(8.2)	19 (3.9)	3(3.2)	5(4.7)	11(6.5)	1(0.8)
	Death	0(0.0)	0(0.0)	8(4.1)	5 (1.0)	4(4.3)	0(0.0)	8(4.7)	2(1.5)
	Bleeding	2(3.9)	0(0.0)	19(9.7)	7 (1.4)	9(9.6)	5(4.7)	10(5.9)	1(0.8)
	Mysterious illness	1(2.0)	5(5.2)	6(3.1)	12 (2.4)	1(1.1)	7(6.6)	2(1.2)	2(1.5)
	Mystery	0(0.0)	3(3.1)	0(0.0)	17 (3.4)	0(0.0)	1(0.9)	0(0.0)	6(4.6)
	Virulent	0(0.0)	2(2.1)	2(1.0)	6 (1.2)	1(1.1)	1(0.9)	0(0.0)	4(3.1)

Themes	Key Words	National Post		Hamilton Spectator		Globe and Mail		Toronto Star	
		N₁ (%)	N₂ (%)	N₁ (%)	N₂ (%)	N₁ (%)	N₂ (%)	N₁ (%)	N₂ (%)
Identity	Congolese woman	0(0.)	8(8.2)	8(4.1)	23 (4.7)	3(3.2)	11(10.4)	7(4.1)	8(6.1)
	Congo	7(13.7)	5(5.2)	10(5.1)	35 (7.1)	10(10.6)	6(5.7)	9(5.3)	8(6.1)
	Congolese	0(0.0)	1(1.0)	0(0.0)	10 (2.0)	2(2.1)	0(0.0)	0(0.0)	2(1.5)
	Africa	3(5.9)	2(2.1)	14(7.1)	19 (3.9)	6(6.4)	3(2.8)	11(6.5)	4(3.1)
	Naming	0(0.0)	10(10.3)	0(0.0)	107 (21.7)	8(8.5)	33(31.1)	0(0.0)	20(15.3)
Suspicion/ Crime	Investigation/ Smuggling	0(0.0)	13(13.4)	0(0.0)	24 (4.9)	1(1.1)	5(4.7)	0(0.0)	3(2.3)
Immigration	Visitor's status	1(2.0)	11(11.3)	3(1.5)	34 (6.9)	0(0.0)	5(4.7)	10(5.9)	10(7.6)
	Screening	1(2.0)	1(1.0)	0(0.0)	1 (0.2)	0(0.0)	0(0.0)	7(4.1)	0(0.0)
	Immigration	0(0.0)	10(10.3)	2(1.0)	13 (2.6)	2(2.1)	2(1.9)	11(6.5)	3(2.3)
Total		51(100)	97(100)	196(100)	493(100)	94(100)	106(100)	169 (100)	131(100)

N₁ denotes the frequencies of words in the newspaper articles in the Ebola period: February 6–8, 2001. N₂ denotes the frequencies of key words in the newspaper articles in the Post-Ebola period: February 9 to March 7, 2001.

Key Words in the Newspapers' Headlines

Key Words	National Post		Hamilton Spectator		Globe and Mail		Toronto Star	
	N_1 (%)	N_2 (%)	N_1 (%)	N_2 (%)	N_1 (%)	N_2 (%)	N_1 (%)	N_2 (%)
Ebola	4(40)	6(31.6)	3(16.7)	11(39.3)	5(55.6)	2(18.2)	5(33.3)	3(33.3)
Deadly	1(10)	1(5.3)	3(16.7)	1(3.6)	1(11.1)	2(18.2)	1(6.7)	0(0)
Risk	1(10)	1(5.3)	1(5.6)	2(7.1)	1(11.1)	0(0)	0(0)	0(0)
Congo	0(0)	1(5.3)	1(5.6)	3(10.7)	1(11.1)	0(0)	0(0)	0(0)
Congolese woman	0(0)	1(5.3)	0(0)	6(21.4)	0(0)	3(27.3)	1(6.7)	2(22.2)
Mystery	1(10)	5(26.3)	1(5.6)	3(10.7)	0(0)	2(18.2)	1(6.7)	2(22.2)
Virus	3(30)	1(5.3)	3(16.7)	1(3.6)	1(11.1)	2(18.2)	5(33.3)	1(11.1)
***Other	0(0)	3(15.8)	6(33.3)	1(3.6)	0(0)	0(0)	2(13.3)	1(11.1)
Total	10(100)	19(100)	18(100)	28(100)	9(100)	11(100)	15(100)	9(100)

N_1 denotes the frequencies of words in the newspaper headlines in the Ebola period: February 6– 8, 2001.

N_2 denotes the frequencies of key words in the newspaper headlines in the post-Ebola period: February 9, 2001 to March 7, 2001.

***Other: This category is determined by empty cells that are more than four. They are smuggling/investigation, mysterious, dangerous, bleeding and crisis.

Frequency of News Reports with Quoted Sources

Source	National Post		Hamilton Spectator		Globe and Mail		Toronto Star	
	N_1 (%)	N_2 (%)	N_1 (%)	N_2 (%)	N_1 (%)	N_2 (%)	N_1 (%)	N_2 (%)
Doctors	10(66.7)	6(35.3)	34(54.8)	60(40.3)	12(63.2)	7(46.7)	19(46.3)	16(57.1)
*Experts	0(0)	0(0)	1(1.6)	8(5.4)	0(0)	0(0)	1(2.4)	1(3.6)
**Govt. officials	0(0)	4(23.5)	5(8.1)	20(13.4)	2(10.5)	2(13.3)	15(36.6)	0(0)
Union leaders	3(20.0)	1(5.9)	13(21.0)	4(2.7)	1(5.3)	1(6.7)	1(2.4)	4(14.3)
***Blacks	0(0)	2(11.8)	2(3.2)	27(18.1)	0(0)	0(0)	1(2.4)	4(14.3)
Hosp. Staff	2(13.3)	4(23.5)	4(6.5)	17(11.4)	3(15.8)	5(33.3)	2(4.9)	1(3.6)
****Other	0(0.0)	0(0.0)	3(4.8)	13(8.7)	1(5.3)	0(0.0)	2(4.9)	2(7.1)
Total	15(100)	17(100)	62(100)	149(100)	19(100)	15(100)	41(100)	28(100)

N_1 denotes quoted sources in the newspaper articles in the Ebola period: from February 6, 2001 to February 8, 2001.

N_2 denotes quoted sources in the newspaper articles in the Post-Ebola period: from February 9, 2001 to March 7, 2001.

*Experts: university professors.

**Government officials: Spokespersons for the Centres for Disease Control, Immigration and Citizenship Canada officials, Canada customs; police officers, government ministers and the staff of Canada Customs.

***Blacks: these are mainly Congolese.

****Other: Air Canada, SISSO, ABC and the Congolese embassy official.

References

Achebe, Chinua. 1989. "An Image of Africa: Racism in Conrad's *Heart of Darkness.*" In *Hopes and Impediments: Selected Essays*. New York: Doubleday: 1–20.

Adeyanju, Charles. 2006. "Yoruba-Nigerians in Toronto: Transnational Practices and Experiences." In Ann Genova and Toyin Falola (eds.), *Yoruba Identity and Power Politics*, Rochester: University of Rochester Press: 251–72.

——— and Nicole Neverson. 2007. "There Will Be A Next Time": Media Discourse about an "Apocalyptic" Vision of Immigration, Racial Diversity, and Health Risks." *Canadian Ethnic Studies* 39 (1 & 2): 79–105.

Akioye, Akin. 1994. "The Rhetorical Construction of Radical Africanism at the United Nations: Metaphoric Cluster as Strategy." *Discourse & Society* 5 (1): 7–31.

Ali, S. Harris, and Roger Kiel. 2006. "Global Cities and the Spread of Infectious Disease: The Case of Severe Acute Respiratory Syndrome (SARS) in Toronto, Canada." *Urban Studies* 43 (3): 491–509.

Altheide, L. David. 2002. *Creating Fear: News and the Construction of Crisis*. New York: Aldine De Gruyter.

Althusser, Louis. 1971. "Ideology and Ideological State Apparatuses." In *Lenin and Philosophy*. London: New Left Books.

Arat-Koc, Sedef. 2005. "The Politics of Family and Immigration in the Subordination of Domestic Workers in Canada." In Valerie Zawilski and Cynthis Levine-Rasky (eds.), *Inequality in Canada: A Reader on the Intersections of Gender, Race, and Class*, Don Mills, ON: Oxford University Press: 363–84.

Astroff, J. Roberta, and Amy K. Nyberg. 1992. "Discursive Hierarchies and the Construction of Crisis in the News: A Case Study." *Discourse & Society* 3 (1): 5–23.

Austin, Sydney. 1990. "AIDS and Africa: United States Media and Racist Fantasy." *Cultural Critique* Winter 1989-90: 129–52.

Bahdi, Reem. 2003. "No Exit: Racial Profiling and Canada's War Against Terrorism." *Osgoode Hall Law Journal* 41: 293–317.

Balibar, Etienne. 1991. "Is there a 'Neo-Racism?'" In Etienne Balibar and Immanuel Wallerstein (eds.), *Race, Nation, Class: Ambiguous Identities*. London: Verso: 17–28.

Barker, Martin. 1981. *The New Racism: Conservatives and the Ideology of the Tribe*. London: Junction Books.

Barrett, Stanley. 1994. *Paradise: Class, Commuters, and Ethnicity in Rural Ontario*. Toronto: University of Toronto Press.

_____. 1987. *Is God a Racist? The Right Wing in Canada*. Toronto: University of Toronto Press.

_____. 1984. "White Supremacists and Neo-Fascists: Laboratories for the Analysis of Racism in Wider Society." *Canadian Ethnic Studies* 16 (1): 1–15.

Barthes, Roland. 1972. "Myth Today." In *Mythologies* London: Cape.

Basch, L., Nina Glick-Schiller, and C.S. Blanc. 1994. *Nations Unbound*. New York: Gorden and Breach.

Beck, Ulrich. 1998. *Democracy Without Enemies*. Cambridge: Polity Press.

_____. 1992. *Risk Society: Towards a New Modernity*. New York: Sage.

Becker, Howard. 1967. "Whose Side Are We On?" *Social Problems* 14 (3) (Winter): 239–47.

Berger, Peter. 1992. "Sociology as a Form of Consciousness." In Candace Clark and Howard Robboy (eds.), *Social Interaction: Readings in Sociology*. Fourth edition. New York: St. Martin's Press: 6–23.

Bolaria, Singh, and Peter Li. 1985. *Racial Oppression in Canada*. Toronto: Garamond Press.

Bourdieu, P. 1984. *Distinction: A Social Critique of the Judgment of Taste*. Translated by Richard Nice. Cambridge, MA: Harvard University Press.

Breton, Raymond. 1964. "Institutional Completeness of Ethnic Communities and the Personal Relations of Immigrants." *American Journal of Sociology* 70: 103–205.

Brookes, J. Heather. 1995. "'Suit, Tie and a Touch of Juju' — The Ideological Construction of Africa: A Critical Discourse Analysis of News on Africa in the British Press." *Discourse & Society* 6 (4): 461–94.

Brown, Julianne, Simon Chapman and Deborah Lupton. 1996. "Infinitesimal Risk as Public Health Crisis: News Media Coverage of a Doctor-Patient HIV Contact Tracing Investigation." *Social Science Medicine* 43 (12): 1685–95.

Bryman, Alan. 2004. *Social Research Methods*. Second edition. Oxford: Oxford University Press

Carroll, William, and R.S. Ratner. 1999. "Media Strategies and Political Projects: A Comparative Study of Social Movements." *Canadian Journal of Sociology* 24 (1): 1–34.

Cashmore, E. Ellis. 1990. "The Functions of Racial Conflict." *The European Journal of Intercultural Studies* 1 (1): 7–20.

Chavez, Leo. 1994. "The Power of Imagined Community: The Settlement of Undocumented Mexicans and Central Americans in the United States." *American Anthropologist* 96 (1): 52–73.

Chirimuuta, Richard, and Rosalid Chirimuuta. 1989. *AIDS, Africa and Racism*. London: Free Association Books.

Cohen, Stanley. 1972. *Folk Devils and Moral Panics: The Creation of the Mods and Rockers*. London: MacGibbon and Kee.

Conrad, Joseph. 1950. *Heart of Darkness and the Secret Sharer*. New York: New York American Library.

Cooley, Charles Horton. 1962. *Social Organization*. New York: Schocken Books.

Coser, Lewis. 1956. *The Functions of Social Conflict*. Glencoe: Free Press.

Cox, Oliver. 1948. *Caste, Class and Race*. Garden City: Doubleday.

Creese, G., and L. Peterson. 1996. "Making the News, Racializing Chinese Canadians." *Studies in Political Economy* 51: 117–46.

Critcher, Chas. 2003. *Moral Panics and the Media*. Buckingham: Open University Press.

_____. 2002. "Media, Government and Moral Panic: The Politics of Paedophilia in Britain 2000–1." *Journalism Studies* 3 (4): 521–35.

De Cillia, Rudolf, Martin Reisigl and Ruth Wodak. 1999. "The Discursive Construction of National Identities." *Discourse & Society* 10 (2): 149–73.

Dew, Kevin. 1999. "Epidemics, Panic and Power: Representations of Measles and Measles Vaccines." *Health* 3 (4): 379–98.

Dua, Enakshi. 2007. "Exploring Articulations of 'Race' and Gender: Going Beyond Singular Categories." In Hier Sean and Singh Bolaria (eds.), *Race & Racism in the 21st-Century Canada: Continuity, Complexity, and Change*. Peterborough, ON: Broadview Press: 175–96.

_____. 2000. "The Hindu Woman's Question: Canadian Nation-Building and the Social Construction of Gender for South Asian-Canadian Women." In A. Calliste and Dei George (eds.), *Anti-Racist Feminism*. Halifax: Fernwood.

Dubois, Laurent. 1996. "A Spoonful of Blood: Haitians, Racism and AIDS." *Science as Culture* 6 (1): 7–43.

Entman, Robert. 1993. "Framing: Toward Clarification of a Fractured Paradigm." *Journal of Communication* 43, 4 (Autumn): 51–58.

Etoroma, Efajemue. 1992. "Blacks in Hamilton: An Analysis of Factors in Community Building." Unpublished Ph.D. thesis, Hamilton: McMaster University.

Fairclough, Norman. 1998. "Political Discourse in the Media: An Analytical Framework." In Allan Bell and Peter Garrett (eds.), *Approaches to Media Discourse*. Oxford: Blackwell Publishers: 142–62.

Fanon, Frantz. 1967. *Black Skin, White Masks*. New York: Grove Press, Inc.

Fiske, J. 2000. "White Watch." In Cottle Simon (ed.), *Ethnic Minorities and the Media*. Buckingham: Open University Press: 50–66.

_____. 1996. *Media Matters: Everyday Culture and Political Change*. Minneapolis: University of Minnesota Press.

Fleras, Augie. 1994. "Media and Minorities in a Post-Multicultural Society: Overview and Appraisal." In J.W. Berry and J.A. Laponce (eds.), *Ethnicity and Culture in Canada*. Toronto: University of Toronto Press.

_____. 2003. *Mass Media Communication in Canada*. Toronto: Thomson Nelson.

Fleras, Augie, and Leonard Elliot. 2003. *Unequal Relations: An Introduction to Race and Ethnic Dynamics in Canada*. Fourth edition. Toronto: Prentice Hall.

Fleras, Augie, and J. Kunz. 2001. *Media and Minorities: Representing Minorities in Multicultural Canada*. Toronto: Thomson Educational Publishing.

Foucault, Michel. 1980. "Truth and Power." In *Power/Knowledge*. New York: Pantheon.

Frakenberg, Ruth. 1993. *The Social Construction of Whiteness: White Women, Race Matters*. Minneapolis: University of Minnesota Press.

Fraser, Nancy. 2005. "Reframing Justice in a Globalizing World." *New Left Review* 36: 69–88.

_____. 2000. "Rethinking Recognition." *New Left Review* 3: 107–20.

_____. 1996. "Rethinking the Public Sphere: A Contribution to the Critique of Actually Existing Democracy." In C. Calhoun (ed.), *Habermas and the Public Sphere*. Cambridge: MIT Press.

_____. 1995. "From Redistribution to Recognition? Dilemmas of Justice in a 'Post-Socialist Age.'" *New Left Review* 212: 68–93.

Galabuzi, Grace-Edward. 2006. *Canada's Economic Apartheid: The Social Exclusion of Racialized Groups in the New Century*. Toronto: Canadian Scholars' Press.

Galtung, Johan, and Mari Ruge. 1981. "Structuring and Selecting News." In Stanley Cohen and Jock Young (eds.), *The Manufacturing of News: Social Problems, Deviance and the Mass Media*. London: Constable: 52–63.

Garrett, Laurie. 2000. *Betrayal of Trust: The Collapse of Global Public Health*. New York: Hyperion.

Giddens, Anthony. 1991. *Modernity and Self-Identity: Self and Society in the Late Modern Age*. Stanford: Stanford University Press.

_____. 1990. *The Consequences of Modernity*. Cambridge: Polity Press.

_____. 1984. *The Constitution of Society*. Berkeley: University of California Press.

Gillett, James. 2007. "Internet Web Logs as Cultural Resistance: A Study of the SARS Arts Project." *Journal of Communication Inquiry* 31 (1): 28–43.

Gilman, Sander. 1985. "Black Bodies, White Bodies: Toward an Iconography of Female Sexuality in Late Nineteenth-Century Art, Medicine, and Literature." *Critical Inquiry* 12, 1 (autumn): 204–42.

Gilroy, Paul. 1993. *The Black Atlantic: Modernity and Double Consciousness*. Cambridge: Harvard University Press.

Glick Schiller, Nina, Linda Basch and Cristina Szanton Blanc. 1992. *Towards a Transnationals Perspective on Migration: Race, Class, Ethnicity, and Nationalism Reconsidered*. New York: Annals of the New York Academy of Sciences.

Goffman, Erving. 1963. *Stigma: Notes on the Management of Spoiled Identity.* Englewood Cliffs, NJ: Prentice-Hall.

Goldring, Luin. 1998. "The Power of Status in Transnational Social Fields." In Michael Smith and Luis Guarnizo (eds.), *Transnationalism from Below.* New Brunswick, NJ: Transaction Publishers: 165–95.

_____. 1996. "Blurring Borders: Constructing Transnational Community in the Process of Mexico–US Migration." *Research in Community Sociology* 6: 69–104.

Goode, Erich, and Nachman Ben-Yehuda. 1994. *Moral Panics: The Social Construction of Deviance.* Oxford: Blackwell.

Greenberg, Joshua. 2000. "Opinion Discourse and the Canadian Newspapers: The Case of the Chinese 'Boat People'." *Canadian Journal of Communication* 25 (4): 517–37.

Greenberg, Joshua, and Sean Hier. 2001. "Crisis, Mobilization and Collective Problematization: 'Illegal' Chinese Migrants and the Canadian News Media." *Journalism Studies* 2 (4): 563–83.

Greenberg, Joshua, and Graham Knight. 2004. "Framing Sweatshops: Nike, Global Production, and the American News Media." *Communication and Critical/Cultural Studies* 1 (2): 151–75.

Greenberg, Joshua, and Brian Wilson 2006. "Youth Violence, Moral Panic, and the Canadian Media News Coverage of School Shootings in the United States and Canada." In P. Attallah and L.R. Shade (eds.), *MediaScapes: New Patterns in Canadian Communication.* Toronto: Thomson-Nelson: 95–113.

Gwyn, Richard. 1999. "'Killer Bugs', 'Silly Buggers' and 'Politically Correct Pals': Competing Discourses in Health Scare Reporting." *Health* 3 (3): 335–46. Sage Journals Online

Habermas, J. 1981. *The Theory of Communicative Action.* London: Beacon Press.

Hall, S. 1997. "The Spectacle of the 'Other.'" In Stuart Hall (ed.), *Representation: Cultural Representations and Signifying Practices.* London: The Open University Press: 223–90.

_____. 1996. *Race, the Floating Signifier.* Video. Northampton: Media Education Foundation.

_____. 1992. "The Question of Cultural Identity." In Stuart Hall, David Held and Tony McGrew (eds.), *Modernity and its Futures.* Cambridge: Open University: 273–325.

_____. 1981. "The Whites of Their Eyes: Racist Ideologies and the Media." In George Bridges and Rosalind Brunt (eds.), *Silver Linings: Some Strategies for the Eighties.* London: Lawrence and Wishart: 7–23.

_____. 1980. "Encoding/Decoding." In Stuart Hall (ed.), *Culture, Media, Language, Working Papers in Cultural Studies.* UK: Hutchinson: 128–38.

_____. 1977. "Culture, the Media and the Ideological Effect." In James Curran, Michael Gurevitch and Janet Woollacott (eds.), *Mass Communication and Society.* London: Edward Arnold: 315–48.

Hall, Stuart, Chas Critcher, Tony Jefferson, John Clarke and Brian Roberts. 1978. *Policing the Crisis: Mugging, the State, and Law-and-order.* London: Macmillan.

Hamilton, L. David, and Tina K. Trolier. 1986. "Stereotypes and Stereotyping: An Overview of the Cognitive Approach." In John Dovidio and Samuel L. Gaertner (eds.), *Prejudice, Discrimination, and Racism.* Orlando: Academic Press: 127–63.

Hay, Colin. 1996. "Narrating Crisis: The Discursive Construction of the 'Winter of Discontent'." *Sociology* 30 (2): 253–77.

Henry, Frances. 2006. "A Response to Hier and Walby's Article: Competing Analytical Paradigms in the Sociological Study of Racism in Canada." *Canadian Ethnic Studies* 38 (2): 169–73.

Henry, Frances, and Carol Tator. 2006. *The Colour of Democracy: Racism in Canadian Society.*

Second edition. Toronto: Thomson-Nelson.

_____. 2002. *Discourses of Domination: Racial Bias in the Canadian English-Language Press.* Toronto: University of Toronto Press.

Hier, Sean. 2003. "Risk and Panic in Late Modernity: Implications of the Converging Sites of Social Anxiety." *The British Journal of Sociology* 54 (1): 3–20.

_____. 2002a. "Raves, Risks and the Ecstacy Panic: A Case Study in the Subversive Nature of Moral Regulation." *Canadian Journal of Sociology* 27 (1): 33–57.

_____. 2002b. "Conceptualizing Moral Panic through a Moral Economy of Harm." *Critical Sociology* 28 (3): 311–34.

_____. 2000. "The Contemporary Structure of Canadian Racial Supremacism: Networks, Strategies and New Technologies." *Canadian Journal of Sociology* 25 (4): 471–94.

Hier, Sean, and Joshua Greenberg. 2002. "Constructing a Discursive Crisis: Risk, Problematization and Illegal Chinese in Canada." *Ethnic and Racial Studies* 25 (3): 490–513.

Hollway, Wendy, and Tony Jefferson. 1997. "The Risk Society in an Age of Anxiety: Situating Fear of Crime." *British Journal of Sociology* 48 (2): 255–66.

Horkheimer, M., and T. Adorno. 1982. "The Culture Industry: Enlightenment as Mass Deception." In *The Dialectic of Enlightenment.* NY: Continuum.

Howard-Hassmann, Rhoda. 1999. "'Canadian' as Ethnic Category: Implications for Multiculturalism and National Unity." *Canadian Public Policy* 25 (4): 523–37.

Husbands, Christopher. 1994. "Crises of National Identity as the 'New Moral Panics': Political Agenda-Setting about Definitions of Nationhood." *New Community* 20 (2): 191–206.

Isaac, Harold. 1975. "Basic Group Identity: The Idols of the Tribe." In Glazer Nathan and Daniel P. Moynihan (eds.), *Ethnicity: Theory and Experience.* Cambridge: Harvard University Press: 29–52.

Jhappan, Radha. 1996. "Post-Modern Race and Gender Essentialism or a Post-Mortem of Scholarship." *Studies in Political Economy* 51: 15–63.

Jiwani, Yasmin. 2006. *Discourses of Denial Mediations of Race, Gender, and Violence.* Vancouver: UBC Press.

_____. 2005. "The Great White North Encounters September 11: Race, Gender, and Nation in Canada's National Daily, the *Globe and Mail.*" *Social Justice* 32 (4): 50–68.

Joffe, Helene, and Georgina Haarhoff. 2002. "Representations of Far-Flung Illness: The Case of Ebola in Britain." *Social Science & Medicine* 54: 955–69.

Kallen, Evelyn. 1995. *Ethnicity and Human Rights in Canada.* Second edition. Toronto: Oxford University Press.

Kitzinger, Jenny. 1998a. "Media Impact on Public Beliefs about AIDS." In David Miller, Jenny Kitzinger, Kevin Williams and Peter Beharrell (eds.), *The Circuit of Mass Communication.* London: Sage: 167–91.

_____. 1998b. "Resisting the Message: The Extent and Limits of Media Influence." In David Miller, Jenny Kitzinger, Kevin Williams and Peter Beharrell (eds.), *The Circuit of Mass Communication.* London: Sage: 192–212.

Knight, Graham. 2004. "The Mass Media." In Robert J. Brym (ed.), *New Society: Sociology for the 21st Century.* Fourth edition. Toronto: Thomson Nelson: 127–53.

_____. 2001. "Prospective News: Press Pre-framing of the 1996 Ontario Public Service Strike." *Journalism Studies* 2 (1): 73–91.

_____. 1998a. "Hegemony, the Media, and New Right Politics: Ontario in the Late 1990s." *Critical Sociology* 24 (1/2): 105–29.

_____. 1998b. "The Mass Media." In Robert Brym (ed.), *New Society: Sociology for the 21st*

Century. Second edition. Toronto: Harcourt Brace Canada: 103–27.

_____. 1982. "News and Ideology." *Canadian Journal of Communication* 8 (4): 15–41.

Knowles, Valerie. 1997. *Strangers at Our Gates: Canadian Immigration and Immigration Policy, 1540–1997*. Toronto: Dundurn Press.

Lavani, Suren. 1995. "Consuming the Exotic Other." *Critical Studies in Mass Communication* 12 (3): 263–86.

Li, Peter. 2003. *Destination Canada: Immigration Debates and Issues*. Oxford: Oxford University Press.

_____. 2001. "The Racial Subtext in Canada's Immigration Discourse." *Journal of International Migration and Integration* 2 (1): 77–97.

_____. 1998. "The Market Value and Social Value of Race." In Vic Satzewich (ed.), *Racism and Social Inequality in Canada*. Toronto: Thompson Educational Publishing: 115–30.

_____. 1995. "Racial Supremacism Under Social Democracy." *Canadian Ethnic Studies* 27 (1): 1–17.

Lian, Jason, and David Mathews. 1998. "Does the Vertical Mosaic Still Exist? Ethnicity and Income in Canada, 1991." *The Canadian Review of Sociology and Anthropology* 35 (4).

Livingstone, David, and Marshall Mangan. 1996. "Introduction: The Changing Context of Class and Gender Relations in Contemporary Canada." In David Livingstone and Marshall Mangan (eds.), *Recast Dreams: Class and Gender Consciousness in Steeltown*. Toronto: Garamond Press: 1–14.

Loeb, Mark, Douglas MacPherson, Michele Barton and Jan Olde. 2003. "Implementation of the Canadian Contingency Plan for a Case of Suspected Viral Hemorrhagic Fever." *Infection Control and Hospital Epidemiology* 24 (4): 280–83.

Loseke, Donileen. 2003. *Thinking About Social Problems*. Second edition. New York: Aldine De Gruyter.

Lupton, Deborah. 1999. *Risk*. London: Routledge.

Lupton, Deborah, and Jane McLean. 1998. "Representing Doctors: Discourses and Images in the Australian Press." *Social Science and Medicine* 46 (8): 947–58.

Lupton, Deborah, and John Tulloch. 2001. "Border Crossings: Narratives of Movement, 'Home' and 'Risk'." *Sociological Research Online* 5 (4). Available at <http://www.socresonline.org.uk/5/4/lupton.html> accessed April 03, 2009.

Ma, Jianming, and Kai Hildebrandt. 1993. "Canadian Press Coverage of the Ethnic Chinese Community: A Content Analysis of the *Toronto* and the *Vancouver Sun*, 1970–1990." *Canadian journal of Communication* 18: 479–96.

Mandela, Nelson. 1994. *Long Walk to Freedom: The Autobiography of Nelson Mandela*. Boston: Little, Brown.

Manoni, Octave. 1964. *Prospero and Caliban: The Psychology of Colonization*. New York: Frederick A. Praeger.

Mawani, Renisa. 2002. "Regulating the 'Respectable' Classes: Venereal Disease, Gender, and Public Health Initiatives in Canada, 1914–35." In John McLaren, Dorothy Chunn, and Robert Menzies (eds.), *Regulatory Lives: Historical Essays on the State, Society, the Individual, and the Law*. Vancouver: UBC Press: 170–95.

McLaughlin, Neil. 2001. "Optimal Marginality: Innovation and Orthodoxy in Fromm's Revision of Psychoanalysis." *The Sociological Quarterly* 42 (2): 271–88.

McRobbie, Angela. 1994. "Folk Devils Fight Back." *New Left Review* 203: 107–16.

McRobbie, Angela, and Sarah L. Thornton. 1995. "Rethinking 'Moral Panic' for Multi-Mediated Social Worlds." *British Journal of Sociology* 46 (4): 559–74.

Mensah, Joseph. 2002. *Black Canadians: History, Experience, Social Condition*. Halifax: Fernwood Publishing.

Miles, Robert. 1989. *Racism.* London: Routledge.

_____. 1988. "Beyond the 'Race' Concept: The Reproduction of Racism in England." In Marie de Lepervanche and Gillian Bottomley (eds.), *The Cultural Construction of Race.* Sydney: University of Sydney Press: 7–31.

Miles, Robert, and Malcolm Brown. 2003. *Racism.* Second edition. London: Routledge.

Miles, Robert, and Vic Satzewich. 1990. "Migration, Racism and 'Postmodern' Capitalism." *Economy and Society* 19 (3): 334–58.

Miller, David. 1999. "Risk, Science and Policy: Definitional Struggles, Information Management, the Media and BSE." *Social Science & Medicine* 49: 1239–55.

Mills, Wright. 1956. *The Power Elite.* New York: Oxford University Press.

Murdocca, Carmela. 2003. "When Ebola Came to Canada: Race and the Making of the Respectable Body." *Atlantis* 27 (2): 24–31.

Murray, Susan. 2001. "When Scratch Becomes 'a Scary Story': The Social Construction of Micro Panics in Center-Based Child Care." *The Sociological Review* 49 (4): 512–29.

Nagel, Joane. 1994. "Constructing Ethnicity, Creating and Recreating Ethnic Identity and Culture." *Social Problems* 41 (1): 57–71.

Olzak, Susan. 1983. "Contemporary Ethnic Mobilization." *Annual Review of Sociology* 9: 355–74.

Oriola, Temitope, and Charles Adeyanju. 2009. "Hunted: The Symbolism of the Noose." *African Identities* 7 (1): 89–103.

Ornstein, Michael. 2000. *Ethno-Racial Inequality in the City of Toronto: An Analysis of the 1996 Census.* Toronto: Center of Excellence for Research on Immigration and Settlement.

Persson, Asha, Kane Race and Elisabeth Wakeford. 2003. "HIV Health in Context: Negotiating Medical Technology and Lived Experience." *Health: An Interdisciplinary Journal for the Social Study of Health, Illness and Medicine* 7 (4): 397–415.

Pieterse, Jan Nederveen. 1992. *White on Black: Images of Africa and Blacks in Western Popular Culture.* New Haven: Yale University Press.

Porter, John. 1965. *The Vertical Mosaic.* Toronto: University of Toronto Press.

Poulantzas, Nicos. 1978. *Classes in Contemporary Capitalism.* London: Verso.

Power, J. Gerard. 1995. "Media Dependency, Bubonic Plague, and the Social Construction of the Chinese Other." *Journal of Communication Inquiry* 19, 1 (Spring): 89–110.

Pratt, Anna, and Mariana Valverde. 2002. "From Deserving Victims to 'Masters of Confusion': Redefining Refugees in the 1990s." *Canadian Journal of Sociology* 27 (2): 135–61.

Razack, Sherene. 2004. *Dark Threats and White Knights: The Somalia Affair, Peacekeeping, and the New Imperialism.* Toronto: University of Toronto Press.

Richmond, H. Anthony. 1994. *Global Apartheid: Refugees, Racism, and the New World Order.* Toronto: Oxford University Press.

Ritzer, George. 2007. *Contemporary Sociological Theory and its Classical Roots: The Basics.* Second edition. New York: McGraw Hill.

Rose, William. 2002. "Crimes of Color: Risk, Profiling, and the Contemporary Racialization of Social Control." *International Journal of Politics, Culture and Society* 16 (2): 179–205.

Rowe, David. 1984. "Media Beat Up Migrants: News Values on the Small Screen." *Journal of Intercultural Studies* 5 (1): 5–21.

Sanders, Todd. 2005. "The Torso in the Thames: Imagining Darkest Africa in the United Kingdom." In Anne Meneloy and Donna Young (eds.), *Auto-Ethnographies: The Anthropology and Academic Practices.* Toronto: University of Toronto Press: 126–42.

Satzewich, Vic. 2000. "Whiteness Limited: Racialization and the Social Construction of

'Peripheral Europeans'." *Social History* 33 (66): 271–89.

———. 1998a. "Race and Ethnic Relations." In Robert Brym (ed.), *New Society: Sociology for the 21st Century.* Toronto: Harcourt Brace Canada: 215–39.

———. 1998b. "Race, Racism and Racialization: Contested Concepts." In Vic Satzewich (ed.), *Racism and Social Inequality in Canada.* Toronto: Thompson Educational Publishing: 25–45.

———. 1991. *Racism and the Incorporation of Foreign Labour: Farm Labour Migration to Canada since 1945.* London: Routledge.

Scatamburlo-D'Annibale, Valerie, and Paul Boin. 2006. "New Media." In Paul Attallah and Leslie Regan Shade (eds.), *Mediascapes: New Patterns in Canadian Communication.* Second edition. Toronto: Thomson Nelson: 235–49.

Seale, Clive. 2002. *Media and Health.* London: Sage Publications.

Shah, Nayan. 2001. *Contagious Divides: Epidemics and Race in San Francisco's Chinatown.* Berkeley: University of California Press.

Simmons, Alan. 1998a. "Racism and Immigration Policy." In Vic Satzewich (ed.), *Racism and Social Inequality in Canada.* Toronto: Thompson Educational Publishing: 87–114.

———. 1998b. "Globalization and Backlash Racism in the 1990s: The Case of Asian Immigration to Canada." In Eleanor Laquian, Aprodicio Laquian and Terry McGee (eds.), *The Silent Debate: Asian Immigration and Racism in Canada.* Vancouver: University of British Columbia Institute of Asian Research: 29–50.

Singer, Eleanor. 1990. "A Question of Accuracy: How Journalists and Scientists Report Research on Hazards." *Journal of Communication* 40 (4): 102–16.

Skinner, David. 2006. "Alternative Media." In Paul Attallah and Leslie Regan Shade (eds.), *Mediascapes: New Patterns in Canadian Communication.* Second edition. Toronto: Thomson Nelson: 213–29.

Smith, Charles. 2003. "Hamilton at the Crossroads: Antiracism and the Future of the City — 'Lessons Learned' from Community-Based Anti-Racism Institutional Change Initiatives." A report prepared by Charles C. Smith Consulting for Strengthening Hamilton's Community Initiatives.

Smith, Michael, and Luis Guarnizo (eds.). 1998. *Transnationalism from Below.* London: Transaction Publishers.

Sorenson, John. 1990. "Opposition, Exile and Identity: The Eritrean Case." *Journal of Refugee Studies* 3 (4): 298–319.

Stallings, A. Robert. 1990. "Media Discourse and the Social Construction of Risk." *Social Problems* 37 (1): 80–95.

Stubblefield, Anna. 1995. "Racial Identity and Non-Essentialism about Race." *Social Theory and Practice* 21 (3): 341–68.

Tator, Carol, and Frances Henry. 2006. *Racial Profiling in Canada.* Toronto: University of Toronto Press.

Thobani, Sunera. 2000. "Nationalizing Canadians: Bordering Immigrant Women in the Late Twentieth Century." *Canadian Journal of Women and the Law* 12 (2): 279–312.

Thompson, Kenneth. 1998. *Moral Panics.* London: Routledge.

Tilly, Charles. 1997. *Durable Inequality.* Berkeley: University of California Press.

Tokunbo, Ojo. 2006. "Ethnic Print Media in the Multicultural Nation of Canada: A Case Study of the Black Newspaper in Montreal." *Journalism* 7 (3): 343–61.

Tomes, Nancy. 2000. "Public Health Then and Now: The Making of a Germ Panic, Then and Now." *American Journal of Public Health* 90 (2): 191–98.

Tulloch, John, and Deborah Lupton. 2001. "Risk, the Mass Media and Personal Biography: Revisiting Beck's 'Knowledge, Media and information Society'." *European*

Cultural Studies 4 (1): 5–27.

Ungar, Sheldon. 1998. "Hot Crises and Media Reassurance: A Comparison of Emerging Diseases and Ebola Zaire." *British Journal of Sociology* 49 (1): 37–56.

Vallentin, Jeff. 2002. "Managing a Mystery Virus." Hamilton, ON: Canadian Public Relations Society: Accreditation Work Sample Submission.

van Dijk, Teun. 2001. "Critical Discourse Analysis." In Deborah Schiffrin, Deborah Tannen and Heidi E. Hamilton (eds.), *The Handbook of Discourse Analysis.* Oxford: Blackwell Publishers: 352–71.

_____. 2000. "New(s) Racism: A Discourse Analytical Approach." In Simon Cottle (ed.), *Ethnic Minorities and the Media.* Buckingham: Open University Press.

_____. 1993a. "Principles of Critical Discourse." *Discourse & Society* 4 (2): 249–83.

_____. 1993b. *Elite Discourse and Racism.* Newbury Park: Sage Publications.

_____. 1991. *Racism and the Press.* London: Routledge.

Wardle, Claire. 2006. "It Could Happen To You: The Move Towards 'Personal" and 'Societal' Narratives in Newspaper Coverage of Child Murder, 1930–2000." *Journalism Studies* 7 (4): 515–33.

Washer, Peter. 2004. "Representations of SARS in the British Newspapers." *Social Science & Medicine* 59: 2561–71.

Weber, Max. 1968. *Economy and Society.* Roth Guenther and Claus Wittich (eds.). New York: Bedminister Press.

Wilson, Brian. 1997. "'Good Blacks' and 'Bad Blacks': Media Construction of African-American Athletes in Canadian Basketball." *International Review for the Sociology of Sport* 32 (2): 177–89.

Wilson, Brian, and Michael Atkinson. 2005. "Rave and Straightedge, the Virtual and the Real: Exploring Online and Offline Experiences in Canadian Youth Subcultures." *Youth & Society* 36 (3): 276–311.

Wodak, Ruth, and Bernd Matouschek. 1993. "'We Are Dealing with People whose Origins One can Clearly Tell just by Looking': Critical Discourse Analysis and the Study of Neo-Racism in Contemporary Austria." *Discourse & Society* 4 (2): 225–48.

Wynne, Brian. 1996. "May the Sheep Safely Graze? A Reflexive View of the Expert–Lay Knowledge Divide." In S. Lash, B. Szerszinski, and B. Wynne (eds.), *Risk, Environment and Modernity: Towards a New Ecology.* London: Sage: 44–83.

Zong, Li. 1997. "New Racism, Cultural Diversity and the Search for a National Identity." In Andrew Cardozo and Louis Musto (eds.), *The Battle over Multiculturalism: Does it Help or Hinder Canadian Unity?* Volume 1. Ottawa: Pearson-Shoyama Institute: 115–26.

_____. 1994. "Structural and Psychological Dimensions of Racism: Towards an Alternative Perspective." *Canadian Ethnic Studies* 26 (3): 122–34.

Newspaper Articles
Hamilton Spectator

February 6, 2001a. "Ebola virus rare but deadly: No cases reported in North America."

February 6, 2001b. "Mystery virus fells woman, Ebola not ruled out: Woman arrived from the Congo."

February 6, 2001c. "Nurse battled Ugandan epidemic: Car crash more daunting than getting virus."

February 7, 2001a. "Health Canada launches emergency plan as woman in Henderson hospital fights fever that may be Ebola: Fever sparks crisis plan."

February 7, 2001b. "Fellow passengers are cleared of risk: No symptoms mean no contagion."

February 7, 2001c. "Tracking a mysterious illness: A global village makes it difficult to contain a dangerous infectious disease."

February 7, 2001d. "Living in fear — up to 25 members of the Henderson General Hospital staff may have been exposed to a contagious virus. There is also concern that laboratory technicians improperly handled samples before knowing a woman was seriously ill with a possibly deadly infection. They are now living in a state of 'psychological fear.' Hospital staff being monitored."

February 7, 2001e. "Why it is taking so long to confirm the test results?"

February 8, 2001a. "Infection may have spread: At least 18 people under surveillance after contact with mysterious illness."

February 8, 2001b. "Bleeding alarmed physicians: While suspecting malaria, MDs feared something far worse."

February 8, 2001c. "Infection fears for hospital staff: Woman was admitted to Henderson hospital before potentially deadly illness suspected."

February 8, 2001d. "Understanding hemorrhagic fevers."

February 8, 2001e. "Fatal fevers first reported in '76 and spread by rural, tropical tourism."

February 8, 2001f. "Public health: Unwilling pioneers? Global village is more than a catchphrase."

February 9, 2001a. "Fever patient worsens: 70 people may be at risk of illness."

February 9, 2001b. "Woman's host panicked by illness."

February 9, 2001c. "Fever Pitch — Anxiety is mounting for those exposed to a Congolese woman severely ill with a suspected hemorrhagic fever. Some have temporarily moved from their homes to protect their loved ones: 40 Henderson staff now at risk."

February 9, 2001d. "Commercial courier delivered samples."

February 9, 2001e. "Simple precautions aren't taken: Hospital workers fail to wash their hands after handling patients, samples."

February 9, 2001f. "Questions & Answers."

February 9, 2001g. "Ebola scare: We can take some steps."

February 9, 2001h. "Let's start overseas."

February 10, 2001a. "Prevention reduces threat: African outbreaks of hemorrhagic fevers moderated by hygiene measure."

February 10, 2001b. "Fever Story gripped our newsroom."

February 10, 2001c. "Disease mystery unsolved: Doctors are still bewildered by Congolese woman's illness."

February 10, 2001d. "Victim remains a puzzle to public: Foreign Affairs says only it has contacted her family in Africa."

February 10, 2001e. "Hollywood Dramatization — A book which blended a history of Ebola with the story of a similar virus triggered the blockbuster movie Outbreak and a legend was born. The psychosis of fear generated by images from that film prompted the speculation that it was as deadly as the plague... but the reality is totally different: Why Ebola terrifies us all."

February 10, 2001f. "Fever scare brought out the best in health-care staff."

February 12, 2001a. "Congolese question MDs' diagnosis: Lack experience in tropical diseases."

February 12, 2001b. "Racist leaflets given out near hospital: Heritage Front members monitored by police near Henderson Hospital."

February 13, 2001. "Woman's illness still a mystery: Congolese woman remains on life support, but chances for survival are 'good'."

February 14, 2001. "Ebola scare proves a grave reminder for lab techs to wear gloves on the job."

February 16, 2001. "ABC news plans story on Ebola: TV crew expected in Hamilton next week."

February 17, 2001. "Anatomy of Ebola scare in Hamilton."

February 21, 2001. "Illness still a mystery."

February 22, 2001. "Protect minorities, activists plead: Groups want Hamilton to create an antiracism committee."

February 24, 2001. "Congolese woman slowly improving."

February 26, 2001. "'My life is destroyed' Congolese host says: Ebola scare shattered calm."

March 2, 2001a. "Why we need racism committee."

March 2, 2001b. "Hospital goes to patients."

March 5, 2001a. "'Ebola' patient in smuggling probe: Left hospital Friday went into hiding."

March 5, 2001b. "Diamonds pay for Congo's wars."

March 6, 2001. "Congolese woman draws RCMP's interest: Mounties will meet Immigration officials to discuss Hamilton visit."

March 7, 2001. "Congolese woman cleared of suspicion: RCMP meet immigration officials, say no reason for further probe."

March 12, 2001. "African communities acted to limit Ebola spread."

March 13, 2001. "Ebola scare cost HHSC $60,000: Congolese woman had no health insurance."

March 14, 2001. "Visitor health insurance not likely in Canada."

March 20, 2001. "We all have choices: Racism, Stop It!"

March 9, 2002. "Spectator reporter nominated for top newspaper award."

Globe and Mail

February 6, 2001a. "Ebola fever case feared: Woman from Congo in Hamilton hospital."

February 6, 2001b. "Lab doing test for Ebola."

February 7, 2001a. "Ebola-like case sends authorities scrambling."

February 7, 2001b. "Disease fit for a Stephen King thriller: What is so scary about Ebola, aside from lack of a cure, is the horrific way in which it kills."

February 7, 2001c. "Ebola virus often fatal."

February 8, 2001a. "Exposed hospital staff fear deadly illness."

February 8, 2001b. "No great risk of epidemic, doctor says."

February 8, 2001c. "Isolation room desired to stop spread of disease."

February 9, 2001a. "Deadly virus still puzzles MDs."

February 9, 2001b. "Testing continues for cause of illness."

February 9, 2001c. 'Blood sample delayed."

February 10, 2001. "Lab rules out deadly virus: Hospital workers breathe sigh of relief after mystery illness comes back negative for tropical fevers."

February 13, 2001. "Congolese woman's illness may never by (sic) identified."

February 20, 2001. "Woman still critical with mystery illness."

February 22, 2001. "Doctors still baffled by woman's illness."

February 27, 2001. "Congolese woman's condition improves."

March 5, 2001. "Congolese woman released from hospital."

March 7, 2001. "RCMP rule out probe of victim in Ebola scare."

March 14, 2001. "Ontarians leave trail of hospital debts, too: Suspected Ebola victim's tab unpaid, but official says residents also fail to pay up."

National Post

February 6, 2001. "Hamilton doctors test woman for Ebola virus."

February 7, 2001a. "The Virus: An unknown enemy: Ebola is a 'perfect parasite' with no cure."

February 7, 2001b. "Ebola Scare: Deadly virus not ruled out, public told not to panic: Contingency plan in place: About 12 people at risk."

February 8, 2001. "Mystery illness: Health Canada rules out Ebola: Patient improving: But 18 people will still be monitored for symptoms of other diseases."

February 9, 2001a. "Woman with mystery illness on life-support: Condition worsens: At least 70 being monitored for related symptoms."

February 9, 2001b. "Not quite the plague."

February 9, 2001c. "Ebola madness."

February 10, 2001a. "No one at risk from mystery illness in Hamilton, health officials say: Delay in testing of samples for Ebola downplayed."

February 10, 2001b. "Hamilton: More than deadly viruses and smokestacks."

February 13, 2001. "Ontario: Illness may remain in mystery."

February 20, 2001. "Ontario: Congo patient has malaria."

February 24, 2001. "Woman with mystery illness off critical list."

March 3, 2001. "'Ebola' victim investigated for diamond smuggling: Sick woman caused panic."

March 5, 2001. "Congo woman in Ebola scare leaves hospital."

March 7, 2001. "RCMP scraps smuggling investigation of 'Ebola' woman."

March 13, 2001. "Hospital on hook for Ebola scare medical bill: Woman had no coverage."

March 14, 2001. "Ontario: Mystery illness bills unpaid."

Toronto Star

February 6, 2001a. "Doctors fear woman may have Ebola."

February 6, 2001b. "Mystery illness strikes woman."

February 7, 2001a. "Can't 'shrink wrap' borders, Caplan says: Witmer stresses importance of 'safety of the public'."

February 7, 2001b. "Anxious doctors await Ebola verdict: Woman tested for several rare diseases."

February 7, 2001c. "The globalization of the world's deadliest viruses."

February 7, 2001d. "World-class lab handles most sensitive cases."

February 7, 2001e. "Illness undetected on planes, at entries: Border officials, flight crew saw nothing amiss."

February 7, 2001f. "Ebola virus feared as worst of tropical disease family: Hemorrhagic fevers can cause outbreaks in different areas."

February 8, 2001a. "Ebola ruled out in case of woman: Congolese visitor suffering from another disease, tests show."

February 8, 2001b. "Battery of lab tests can detect Ebola virus."

February 8, 2001c. "Woman had high fever on arriving at hospital: Hemorrhagic virus not ruled out by doctors."

February 8, 2001d. "How the Crisis began."

February 9, 2001a. "Outbreaks can be avoided by screening."

February 9, 2001b. "Disease still a riddle as woman fights for life: Patient clinging to life, diagnosis still unknown."

February 10, 2001a. "The real outbreak has been... hype: Hollywood has heightened fears about a virus that's no threat to North America."

February 10, 2001b. "So alone: The patient who sparked the scare: Congolese woman's illness remains mystery, but 70 contacts get the all-clear."

February 12, 2001. "Woman still fighting for life."

February 13, 2001. "Woman with rare illness may survive: Doctors still can't pinpoint cause of mystery disease."

February 16, 2001. "Nightline comes to town."

February 24, 2001. "Congo woman rallies."

March 5, 2001. "Ebola scare woman released from hospital."

March 7, 2001. "No probe in 'Ebola' case."

March 13, 2001. "Ebola scare costly for hospital: Woman leaves $60,000 in unpaid medical bills."

March 14, 2001. "No mandatory insurance."